SPIRIT-LED
EVANGELISM

SPIRIT-LED
EVANGELISM

REACHING THE LOST
THROUGH LOVE AND POWER

CHÉ AHN

Chosen

a division of Baker Publishing Group
Grand Rapids, Michigan

© 2006 by Ché Ahn

Published by Chosen Books
a division of Baker Publishing Group
P.O. Box 6287, Grand Rapids, MI 49516-6287
www.chosenbooks.com

Paperback edition published 2008

ISBN 978-0-8007-9442-2

Previously published under the title *Fire Evangelism*

Printed in the United States of America

The Library of Congress has cataloged the hardcover edition as follows:
Ahn, Ché, 1956-
    Fire evangelism : reaching the lost through love and power / Ché Ahn.
       p.   cm.
    Includes bibliographical references and index.
    ISBN 10: 0-8007-9410-9 (cloth)
    ISBN 978-0-8007-9410-1 (cloth)
    1. Witness bearing (Christianity). 2. Evangelistic work. I. Title.
BV4520.A35 2006
269'.2—dc22   2006001781

To Dr. Rev. Byung Kook Ahn,
my father, pastor, mentor
and a tremendous example
of someone who sacrificed much
for the sake of the Gospel

CONTENTS

Section 4 Power Evangelism

Section 5 Profound Evangelism

Section 6 Purposeful Evangelism

FOREWORD

In this foreword I want to show you why *Spirit-Led Evangelism* is an extremely timely book. It is a strong word from God for the particular season in which we find ourselves today.

Evangelism has not always been front and center on the agenda of the Church. Both before and after the Protestant Reformation, most people first became Christians by being born in a Christian country. Russia became Christian, for example, by a royal decree from King Vladimir in 988 establishing Orthodoxy as the national religion and ordering his subjects to convert immediately. From then on Russians were socialized into the Church by their families and by their communities. (True, soon after the Reformation an Anabaptist movement came along in Europe that urged people to be born again, but for a long time it suffered persecution and remained peripheral to society in general.)

Things began to change when America was settled without a state church, as the European nations had. A Great Awakening came in the 1700s, Jonathan Edwards and George Whitefield preached personal awakening, Methodist circuit riders fanned throughout the frontier and many were saved in revivalist camp meetings.

None of this, however, was evangelism as we know it today.

As Ché Ahn points out later in this book, we are now in apostolic times, or "new apostolic wineskins." My estimate is that we have been living in the second apostolic age since 2001. This means we now recognize the roles of apostles, prophets, evangelists, pastors and teachers, as Ephesians 4:11 says we are supposed to. Historically here is the progression:

- The Church has always recognized the office of teacher.
- The office of pastor began to be recognized at the Protestant Reformation when pastors replaced the traditional office of priest.
- The office of evangelist, which relates directly to this book, began to be recognized only in the mid-1800s with Charles G. Finney. The process of recognizing Finney as an evangelist provoked major controversy and upheaval in the Church because it pulled many leaders out of their theological comfort zones. Most people today are surprised that evangelists, per se, have been with us for only the last 150 years or so.
- The office of prophet began to be recognized in the 1980s.
- The office of apostle began to be recognized in the 1990s.

But back to evangelists. Once Finney struck the spark, the fires of evangelism began burning mostly through high-profile individuals. Dwight L. Moody made citywide evangelism big business by advertising his campaigns, using decision cards at his altar calls and introducing upscale music to enliven the crowd. A succession of evangelists like Gipsy Smith and Billy Sunday followed him. A fresh surge was seen after World War II with the emergence of large evangelistic ministries under preachers such as Billy Graham, T. L. Osborne, Oral Roberts, Bill Bright, Morris Cerullo and Charles E. Fuller.

But have you noticed something in this brief sketch of the history of evangelism?

Evangelism in the minds of most Christians was the job of professional evangelists, just as building homes was the job of general contractors or performing root canals was the job of dentists. Despite the energetic efforts of those like Bill Bright with his Four Spiritual Laws and D. James Kennedy with his Evangelism Explosion, the people of God in general did not take to heart their individual responsibility of actively spreading the Gospel and leading their friends and relatives to Christ. Some, such as a number of soul-winning Baptist or Pentecostal churches, did evangelize, but not too many.

This is what Ché Ahn is passionate to reverse. I love his term *fire evangelism*, because Ché wants to see the fire of evangelism burn not just in the ministries of professional evangelists but in the heart of every believer.

I said that this book was timely. Here is why. I seriously doubt that the Body of Christ in America was ready for fire evangelism before, say, the 21st century. True, fire evangelism has characterized large parts of the world such as Africa and China and Indonesia for some time. Now I believe it is coming to America.

What are apostles, prophets, evangelists, pastors and teachers for? They are "for the equipping of the saints for the work of ministry," as Ephesians 4:12 says (NKJV). But it is only in the second apostolic age that evangelists, for example, have begun to function under the leadership of apostles. Consequently, evangelists can now fulfill their

11

destiny of equipping the saints for their evangelistic ministry with greater effectiveness than ever before.

We are now entering what some have called "the saints movement." This means we will no longer rely on big-name preachers and televangelists, although these should continue to proclaim the Gospel. Rather, the people of God, in the normal course of their lives, will increasingly be the channels through whom the fire of the Holy Spirit blazes for bringing huge numbers to faith in Christ.

How can such a thing happen? *Spirit-Led Evangelism* answers that question. In this book Ché Ahn gives you not only the why but the how. As you read on, your soul will be stirred and you will want to say, "Yes! Count me in on the great movement of the saints!"

C. Peter Wagner, chancellor
Wagner Leadership Institute

ACKNOWLEDGMENTS

Words are too inadequate to express my deepest gratitude to Bessie Watson Rhoades, who has been a dear friend and my personal editor/writer over the past ten years that she has worked with me. Thanks also to Jane Campbell, editorial director of Chosen Books, for being so persistent with me to do a book for your fine publishing house. I appreciate the labors of Ann Weinheimer in being the official editor of this manuscript for Chosen. Finally, I want to thank the most wonderful family a man could have: my wife and best friend, Sue, my four wonderful children, Gabriel, Grace, Joy and Mary, and my son-in-law, Steve, who each have sacrificed and yet blessed me to go to the nations with the Good News of the Kingdom of God. May their reward from our Father be greater than they could ever imagine.

Introduction

I had just finished giving the altar call at a Japanese Baptist church in Los Angeles and people were streaming forward. Some were making a first-time commitment to the Lord; others were rededicating their lives to Christ. I walked among the crowd, making sure that each person had a counselor to talk and pray with.

A striking Japanese woman walked up to me. She did not tell me her name, but said, "I am a news broadcaster from Tokyo. I just flew in this morning. I want to thank you for sharing the Gospel. I have heard the Christian message many times, but this was the first time I fully understood it."

"Great!" I said. "Do you want to become a Christian?"

"No, I don't think I am ready to become a Christian yet," she replied.

"That's okay. Thank you for being open to the Gospel. I hope one day that you will become a Christian."

Her look seemed to express relief. "Thank you for not pressuring me to become a Christian today," she said.

"Well, can I at least pray for you that God will reveal more of Himself to you?"

"Yes, please."

She bowed her head and clasped her hands together. It was obvious she had observed the way many Christians pray and emulated them perfectly. I gently placed my hands over her, barely touching her head, and began to pray. "Father, I pray that you will make Jesus more real to her." The moment I said those words, she fell to the floor. She did not fall with a *bang*, but simply slumped down as if she had fainted. I knew she had not fainted.

The Toronto Blessing revival (named such since the epicenter of renewal evident in many parts of the world was birthed from Toronto Airport Christian Fellowship), which broke out in January 1994, has acquainted many Christians with this historic experience. Like other ministers in the growing renewal, I have seen believers whom I pray for fall to the ground as the Holy Spirit comes upon them. I learned early to have ushers stand behind those receiving prayer in order to catch them as they fell.

This phenomenon has been called various terms over the years by Pentecostal and charismatic Christians. Some call it being "slain in the Spirit," others call it "falling under the Spirit" or "falling under power." This is not a new experience, of course. Revivals of the past under Charles Finney and the Wesleys described these and many other phenomena as the Holy Spirit came in power. The Cane Ridge, Kentucky, revival of 1801 drew an estimated twenty to thirty thousand people. James Finley, a future Methodist circuit rider who observed the revival, described this occurrence: "At one time I saw at least five hundred swept down in a moment as if a battery of a thousand guns had been opened upon them, and then immediately followed shrieks and shouts that rent the very heavens."

Until that day in Los Angeles, I had seen only Christians fall under the power of the Holy Spirit; but now I was watching a non-Christian have that same experience. She lay on the floor for approximately fifteen minutes. Then she got up and staggered back to her seat with that look I have seen so many times. It is a look of total release and relaxation, with a touch of amazement.

The next day I learned more about her experience. I was at home, tending to a barbecue outdoors when, to my surprise, she arrived with the friend who had taken her to the service the night before. She wanted to tell me that Jesus had indeed made Himself real to her, as I had prayed He would. She had experienced the loving power and presence of God. That night her friend shared the Gospel with her, and this time she gave her life to Jesus Christ. Since then, I have seen a number of non-Christians come to know Jesus as their Lord and Savior by experiencing a powerful healing or by similarly being overtaken by the awesome presence of God.

You might call this *power evangelism* along with—a term I cannot help but initiate—*presence evangelism*. When the Holy Spirit revealed Himself in power to that woman that day, He did so with tangible presence—an encounter resulting in her salvation. We are living in such an exciting hour!

This book is about power evangelism, presence evangelism, friendship evangelism, servant evangelism, church-planting evangelism and so much more. It is a book about fire evangelism—the kind of evangelism that engulfs the hearts of men and women with God's passionate desire to bring them into the liberty for which His Son gave His life. I love every kind of evangelism that reaches the lost through God's love and power. Much of who I am as an evangelist has to do with presence and power evangelism. I so value God's gifting His people to move in healing, signs, wonders and other supernatural means to evangelize because those means often allow us an *exponential* harvest as the lost are confronted by a supernatural but loving God.

Time is short. More than three-and-a-half *billion* people have yet to hear the Gospel, and even more still need to be saved! I desire to take advantage of every awesome avenue the Holy Spirit has made available to fulfill the Great Commission.

Not everyone is called to move in the same types of power and presence evangelism that delight me, but all are given diverse gifts (see 1 Corinthians 12:4–6). We are all responsible for sharing our faith. If your heart resonates with mine, I pray that this book will further equip and inspire you. I believe many more people would move in greater power if they only had full knowledge of what God has made available to them. If that is you, then I pray that this book will provide answers and options. We will look at many delightful ways to "drip" with the message of salvation. We will explore the best ways to share your faith and many other practical insights. I believe anyone reading this book will benefit, no matter what his or her evangelistic emphasis.

I wrote this book for everyone who is hungry to be used by God to evangelize. It is a working testimony—practical text filled with illustrations from my life and others' lives. I simply desire to pour out what God poured into me when I was called as an evangelist in 1974.

There is no doubt that God is raising up His Church to bring in the end-time harvest—the greatest and most thrilling harvest ever in history. This is an instruction manual to help equip "the saints for the work of ministry" (Ephesians 4:12, NKJV) so that they can do their part. I cannot help but do mine; I am consumed by the Great Commission. This book is my life's message.

My prayer is that these pages will impart to you not only the principles and mandate of evangelism but also the desire and power to fulfill them. I pray that out of intimacy with our glorious Lord and fueled by His love, you will be compelled to reach the lost and advance the Kingdom for the glory of God—the greatest reward of your temporal life.

Ché Ahn

SECTION 1

OUR PRIORITY

1

FIRST THINGS FIRST

For years I used a simple illustration to emphasize the importance of getting our priorities right in life. I told how, in my rush to get dressed first thing in the morning, I usually put the second button in the first buttonhole. Then, after buttoning the rest of the buttons, I could see that my shirt was out of alignment and that I looked like a nerd because of the first mistake.

The lesson is clear: If we miss the top priority, all other priorities will fail to fall into place. I feel as though I can speak from authority on this subject since I have missed the top button in life at least as many times as I have missed the number one priority. My appeal to you is to avoid making the same mistake by checking with the "owner's manual"— the Bible—on how evangelism is to be approached.

Now no Christian would doubt the biblical importance of evangelism. Yet it may startle you to remember that evangelism is not the *first* priority given us in Scripture. The Great

Commission was not the "first button." Jesus made it easy for us to get this right by giving us clear direction in His Word. He said to "love the LORD your God with all your heart, with all your soul, with all your mind, and with all your strength" (Mark 12:30, NKJV). Along with that, He said to " 'love your neighbor as yourself.' There is no other commandment greater than these" (verse 31, NKJV).

I begin this book on evangelism with a chapter on this "Great Commandment" because *love* is the first button most often overlooked. I am still learning after years and years of serving the Lord that *all* ministry springs from an intimate, ongoing love relationship with God. God created us to have fellowship with Him and enjoy the privilege of being His sons and daughters before He gave us any assignments. Before He gave Adam and Eve the mandate to "have dominion" (Genesis 1:26, NKJV), He created them to have relationship with Him. He wanted to love them and be loved by them. This awesome God of love desires that all of His sons and daughters be part of His family of affection.

The Better Choice

To know the importance of love—that God values our "being" above our "doing"—has been a hard lesson for me to learn. I am definitely a "doer." The moment I wake up, my greatest temptation is to review my mental "to do" list and get busy accomplishing things "for the Lord."

For years I related better to Martha's busy-ness than to Mary's sitting at Jesus' feet. I would read that account in Luke 10 and sympathize completely with Martha. More accurately, I was aggravated that Mary did not help. After all, many preparations needed to be made for Jesus' visit, and Mary just sat there. I totally missed what Jesus was saying in that text. I may have understood it intellectually, but my heart missed the point. As I saw it, there was a world going to hell and no one could justify taking time to sit around worshiping and waiting on the Lord.

Now I understand. That is what Jesus wants first. He wanted intimacy and relationship with His daughters Mary and Martha. He wants that same intimacy and love with you and me. He wants us in the place where we continually choose "one thing": the "good part" (verse 42, NKJV). That one thing is the most important. All else is secondary. Everything meaningful stems from that intimate, personal love relationship with the Lord. That is buttoning the first button first.

The amazing thing is that if we get this right, all of our other priorities fall into place. We will end up attaining what we desire—including great fruitfulness in ministry. Jesus said, "Remain in me, and I will remain in you. No branch can bear fruit by itself; it must remain in the vine. Neither can you bear fruit unless you remain in me" (John 15:4). This is especially true when it comes to evangelism. So many times we move in what I call "unsanctified zeal." We sincerely want to share the Lord's goodness, but we end up burned out or discouraged because we have not learned the secret of abiding in Him. People lose their first love (see Revelation 2:4) and give up. They run out of self-generated energy, so they quit. Understandable, but not necessary.

Yes, Jesus did command us to go and take the Good News to others, but He never intended for us to do so in our own strength, our own way or out of our own souls. For too long we have emphasized manmade programs and style. The Lord intended for us to go and witness out of our oneness with Him. Even of His own ministry Jesus said this: "I tell you the truth, the Son can do nothing by himself; he can do only what he sees his Father doing, because whatever the Father does the Son also does" (John 5:19). He did only what He saw the Father doing. That is what made Jesus' life and ministry successful: He stayed in close communion with His Father. He moved in the Father's love and in the Father's power.

I have learned that lovers indeed make the best servants. The motivation of lovers' hearts sustains them when times get rough. Lovers do not seek the approval of men. They do not have to trump up energy to please the beloved. The fire of love continually propels them. As lovers of the Lord, our fresh fires are enough to carry us forward.

That is why the Great Commandment must precede the Great Commission if we truly want to flourish in evangelism—or anything else in God.

Please note an important caution. The Word says that our hearts are deceptive above all else (see Jeremiah 17:9). We must ask the Holy Spirit to search us continually and make us aware of our motives. The end goal of our love and communion with Jesus must never be for the sake of achievement—even when that achievement is bringing lost souls into the Kingdom. That is selfish and deceptive. If I loved my wife so that she would be a better cook or housekeeper, that is a selfish motivation. I love her . . . period.

In the same way, we do not love God in order to "get." We love God because of who He is and what He has done for us. God is worthy of our worship and deserving of our praise and adoration. Our motive for love must be pure. We cannot accomplish that on our own, however; even the motivation to love must come from God. He can work that purity in your heart if it is not there and you are honest with Him.

God is love, and everything He does is loving. Since He has made us in His image, then that must be His plan for us, too. As we love with pure hearts, we will find others drawn to us to hear the Good News.

The Love of Christ Compels Us

Love God and love others. But note that this command goes far beyond loving those in the Church (although we could use improvement there, too!). There is no question that when Jesus commanded us to love our neighbors as ourselves He was referring to the lost. This is evident in the story of the Good Samaritan, which He gave to illustrate the kind of love we should demonstrate toward others.

The neighbor who acted in love in that parable was not a socially accepted individual. Christ specifically chose an individual that His audience would find offensive in order to drive home the point. He chose a person who would be unlovable and unacceptable precisely because His unconditional love and salvation are available to everyone.

This is the fiery love of Jesus. When this love is demonstrated, it is like a fire that sweeps the unbeliever into His Kingdom. As individuals are transformed by this love, they in turn cannot help but spread this very same fire and share the Good News with others. This is why I use the term *fire evangelism*.

I am especially moved by what Bob Sorge pens in his wonderful book *The Fire of God's Love* (Oasis House Ministries, 1996):

> We are to love the sinners whom God is calling to Himself just as much as we love those who already believe. God is reserving a baptism of love for His last-days Church that will transform her into a fire blaze of passionate concern for the lost. No amount of rejection will be able to extinguish this fire for the lost because the intensity of the fire is in no way regulated by people's responses, but by the love of God being shed abroad in the heart. You can pour as much water on a burning oil well as you might want; you're not going to extinguish the flame because it's being fed by an underground supply. The only way to stop the flame is to cut off the inner supply. Evangelistic efforts fueled by

people's responses are sure to fizzle out; evangelistic fervor that is fueled by God's love from within can face any human or demonic obstacle without diminishment.

When we are truly motivated by a passionate love for Jesus and for all of His children, nothing will stop us from sharing the gift of His love. Out of the Great Commandment comes the Great Commission.

2

BECAUSE OF LOVE

I love Jesus passionately, and I am not ashamed to say so. Because I am so grateful for what He has done for me, I have given my life for the cause of fulfilling the Great Commission. I do not evangelize because I have to, but because I want to. One does not have to be a full-time minister to make this same decision—we all have equal opportunity to live everyday for the sake of the Gospel.

Thus, with the top priority—the Great Commandment—aligned correctly, we can turn to the motive behind evangelism and reasons why evangelism is a high priority for believers. But first, let's define our term.

Evangelism: A Working Definition

Not everyone has the same definition of *evangelism*. I approach the word from what I consider a holistic or total-life perspective. When I became a Christian in 1973, I was a seventeen-year-old Korean hippie. I did not have a clue what *evangelism* meant. I remember asking my dad, a pastor, what evangelism was. And who or what was an evangelist? I will never forget the expression of disbelief on his face.

"You don't know what *evangelism* means?"

"No," I said. "What is it?"

"Evangelism," he said, "is preaching the Gospel."

Immediately I understood what my dad meant. This was ironic. Even though I did not know the formal term, I had, by this definition, been evangelizing almost every day since my conversion.

I find a question arises, however, when we distinguish *evangelism* from *witnessing*. We are all witnesses whether we want to be or not. We witness every day through our words, actions and character. When we name the name of Christ, we are living epistles read by everyone (see 2 Corinthians 3:2–3). Evangelism goes beyond that. While many have differing views, I offer here my working definition of evangelism:

> *Evangelism* is sharing the Good News of the death and resurrection of Jesus Christ in the power and love of the Holy Spirit, so that people give their whole hearts to Jesus Christ as their personal Lord and Savior—leading to baptism in water, an infilling of the Holy Spirit and, ultimately, incorporation into and discipleship in a local church.

I am committed to true conversion and preservation of the harvest. While some people may find this definition too extensive, I have found great biblical support for this model and see sustained success and growth of new believers as a result.

Certainly I understand that not every person with whom you share the Gospel will become a Christian. Others may receive salvation yet not become responsible church members, be filled with the Spirit or even be water baptized. (We know that a person can be saved without water baptism because the repentant thief on the cross next to Jesus joined Him in Paradise.)

I am stating in my definition what I believe to be the *ultimate goal* and *standard* of conversion as I best understand Scripture. I believe this is the goal to which we should set our sights. We will talk a great deal about the process of sharing the Gospel with nonbelievers, leading to their repentance, but I want to stress here that the process of evangelism also includes water baptism, the infilling of the Holy Spirit and incorporation into a local church. Much of my definition comes directly from the book of Acts. I believe that the following passage shows this clearly:

> "Therefore let all Israel be assured of this: God has made this Jesus, whom you crucified, both Lord and Christ."
>
> When the people heard this, they were cut to the heart and said to Peter and the other apostles, "Brothers, what shall we do?"
>
> Peter replied, "Repent and be baptized, every one of you, in the name of Jesus Christ for the forgiveness of your sins. And you will receive the gift of the Holy Spirit. The promise is for you and your children and for all who are far off—for all whom the Lord our God will call."
>
> With many other words he warned them; and he pleaded with them, "Save yourselves from this corrupt generation." Those who accepted his message were baptized, and about three thousand were added to their number that day.
>
> Acts 2:36–41

"Added to their number" means added to the local church. This is one point about which I am particularly passionate. I have seen many people come to Christ only to fall away because they were never incorporated into a church body and the essential support, fellowship and growth it provides.

My thinking has grown dramatically on this point. Today when I invite people to surrender to the Lord in a public meeting, I emphasize commitment to a local church even over the importance of baptism, prayer or reading the Bible. I have discovered that if a person gets involved in a good church, that person will receive water baptism and be discipled in reading the Bible and praying. While some may disagree, in my more than thirty years of ministry and church planting I have found it to be true.

Checking Our Motives

During my years at Fuller Seminary, one of my favorite courses was taught by a visiting professor, Anglican theologian and evangelist Michael Green. What I valued most was its practicality. The lectures on evangelism were outstanding, and then Mr. Green would challenge us to put into practice what we were learning. He sent us off to nearby Pasadena City College for open-air preaching along with personal evangelism. I loved it!

He also taught us what I believe should be our greatest purpose for evangelizing: "They go because they have fallen in love with the great Lover. They go because they have been set free by the great Liberator. They love Him, and they want that love to reach others. It is far too good to keep to themselves" (*Evangelism through the Local Church*, Nelson, 1992).

We learned in the first chapter that love is our top priority. And just as our motivation for loving God and others must remain pure, so must our motivation for evangelism. When we are touched by His love, we find joy in sharing that love. A paraphrase of 1 John 4:19—"I love because He first loved me"—offers the purest motivation for evangelism. It can fuel every believer.

We should never evangelize out of a sense of duty or guilt; nonbelievers are not fooled when we approach them with this mentality. Evangelism is a "get to," not a "have to." Have you ever talked with people who have a new love interest? Do they tell you about it with a sense of duty? No,

I imagine that you can hardly get them to be quiet. How much more shall we share our joy when we speak of the lover of our souls who has redeemed us with so great a salvation! Evangelism is an honor. We have the privilege of taking the message of His love to a hurting world.

When I first came to Christ, I was so amazed that God would reveal His love to me that I could not help but share the Gospel. I had not been trained in any way to evangelize. My first real encounter with Jesus was when I was at a friend's home with a group of guys. We were drinking beer and smoking pot. I was so tired of doing the same thing every day that I was on the verge of burning out on drugs at the age of seventeen. I left the room where everyone was partying and I went to another bedroom. I sat on the bed and began to talk to God.

I distinctly remember what I said. In an audible voice, I cried out, "God, I don't know if You exist. But if You do exist, and what my parents told me as a little boy is true, that You died for my sins and that there is a heaven and a hell, I want You to reveal Yourself to me and reveal the truth to me!"

The moment I uttered those words, the presence of God's love came all over me. I literally felt His warmth and love envelop me. At the very same time, my mind and eyes were opened to the truth of the Gospel. I wept uncontrollably. I was stunned. Revelation flooded me. The first shocking realization to hit me was that the truth of Jesus was always there—in my home, in the church my father pastored—but I had been looking everywhere else, including in Eastern religion. The second shocking thing was that I was very aware that I was not a good person, and yet God was taking the time to reveal His love to me in such a profound way.

My first impulse was to go back into the other room and tell my friends the incredible revelation I had just received. So I marched back to the party and blurted out, "Guys, I found what we are all looking for. It's Jesus. Jesus revealed Himself to me!" I was beaming.

Rather than give the joyous reception I was hoping for, however, the gang looked at me as if I had smoked one toke of pot too many. My best friend simply said, "Ché, you have really flipped out this time. But you will be okay tomorrow." By the grace of God, I was never the same.

In the midst of that smoky, drug-filled apartment, nowhere near a cathedral or an altar, as I was sitting alone in a bedroom, God met me. For the next three days, I could not stop weeping. Waves of God's love so gripped me that I could not help but cry. I began to tell all my friends what was going on even though I was hardly articulate in those early days of my conversion. I have not stopped evangelizing since. Yes, there are seasons of dryness and times when fervency lessens. But soon the overwhelming love of the Lord enlarges my heart again and I find myself eagerly sharing His love with others.

Now I understand why God calls our relationship with Him our "first love" (Revelation 2:4). When you encounter your first love, you cannot keep it quiet. Every thought, every analogy, every conversation, every good report usually winds up relating to that love. With my Jesus, it is exactly the same.

The Place of Priority

I have found that there are three specific reasons why evangelism holds such a high place of priority.

1. Because God Deserves Honor and Glory

God's honor is at stake. We rarely think in these terms, but it is true. His heart is waiting for our acceptance of His love—but also for our acknowledgment of His supremacy.

All too often, though, we focus only on the position of the lost. That is surely a compelling motivation for evangelizing because it echoes the heart of the Father. He loves His children very much. He is not willing that any of us should perish. If we focus on the sinner's need, however, we can easily fall into the snare of what my friend—minister, speaker and author Winkie Pratney—calls "evangelical humanism." Evangelism becomes man-centered instead of God-centered.

Since God is the supreme King and Creator of the universe, His glory and honor come first. The sinner's need *is* crucial, as we know. But we must remember first that God has given His Son the name above every name. It is vital to understand this: The very reason we live is to bring Him the honor and glory He deserves. If we shun this privilege, we shun our Father's love—thereby dishonoring Him and robbing Him of glory. If, however, we acknowledge His position of supremacy, then evangelism follows in natural course. Since we are His chosen vessels, we bless the Father by making His Son known to all men.

2. *Because It Brings God Joy*

I believe that love is proportional to hurt. The more you love a person, the more that person can hurt you. Consider this illustration. If someone off of the street—a total stranger—called you stupid, that would hurt. It would not come close, however, to the wounding you would experience if your mother told you, "You're a very stupid child." You would not just be hurt, you would be devastated. Why? You crave your mother's love and respect. You are her flesh and blood. What she says carries far more weight with you than the words of someone who does not know you.

The same applies to God. When we deny Him or denigrate His name, He is wounded by the rejection. The Bible says that "God is love" (1 John 4:8). God is perfect in love. He loves the world with a perfect and infinite love. He created us in His image because He wanted sons and daughters to love—not servants who have to obey or beings to lord power over. Because God's love is so great, I believe He feels great pain when we refuse to honor Him.

In addition, the pain of seeing His people suffer because of sin is equally great. We see a glimpse of the pain that He feels in Genesis 6:5–6: "The LORD saw how great man's wickedness on the earth had become. . . . The LORD was grieved that he had made man on the earth, and his heart was filled with pain." Think about that for a moment: He hurts when you and I sin. Our Father is wounded when we do not live the life He intended—or when many of His children do not even realize that His good plan is available to them.

If you want to consider the full dimension of His pain, multiply the sins of humanity day after day, year after year, throughout the history of human existence. No wonder Jesus said, "I tell you that in the same way there will be more rejoicing in heaven over one sinner who repents than over ninety-nine righteous persons who do not need to repent" (Luke 15:7).

The Lord repeats this truth in another way for emphasis: "In the same way, I tell you, there is rejoicing in the presence of the angels of God over one sinner who repents" (Luke 15:10). Why are the angels rejoicing? Because every time a person repents and is converted, it brings indescribable joy to the Father's heart. The angels rejoice because Father God is happy. Could there be any greater thrill than to bring joy to the One who gave us breath? Jesus helped us picture this joy in His story of the father's first sight of the returning Prodigal Son. The boy's father runs out to greet him, throws a party for him in spite of his son's sin and expresses gladness of heart that his son is now "alive" (see Luke 15:17–32).

Is it not humbling to know that we can have a part in bringing infinite joy to God Himself? This alone could be enough to prove that evangelism holds a high priority.

3. Because It Was Jesus' Priority

In the beautiful story of how Zacchaeus found salvation, Jesus concludes by saying, "The Son of Man came to seek and to save what was lost" (Luke 19:10). Jesus came to heal the brokenhearted, to set at liberty those who are bound (see Luke 4:18), to destroy the work of the devil (see 1 John 3:8). Many wonderful acts distinguish Christ as the loving God who came in the flesh.

But Christ had no greater purpose for coming than to bring salvation to a dying world. He had no greater desire than to reconcile us with His Father and to give us life more abundant (see John 10:10). There are two aspects here that propel me into the realization that if this was Jesus' costly priority, it should be ours as well.

The first aspect is that Jesus underwent extreme suffering to save the lost. He did this ultimately by dying a horrendous death on the cross. While most of us have probably seen Mel Gibson's incredible movie depiction of this event, *The Passion of the Christ*, we still can never fathom the intensity of the physical torture this death entailed. Medical doctors have written extensive analyses of Jesus' torture and death, concluding that it was most likely the worst form of human agony and suffering possible.

The second aspect is that beyond the physical pain Jesus endured, I believe He suffered something even worse: the emotional pain of separation. Anyone who has suffered a great loss, say the death of a loved one or a heart-wrenching divorce, knows this pain. But there is nothing that can match the degree of the pain of being separated forever from the One who created you.

I believe that is why Jesus was so willing to accept physical pain upon the cross. He never wanted anyone to have to endure the emotional devastation of separation from the Father. When He cried out, "If there be any other way, let this cup pass from Me" (see Luke 22:42), I believe His concerns were about far more than temporal, physical distress. He knew that would end. But He had never been separated in all eternity from the love of the Father, and that severing was a far more torturous death.

There is no greater pain and loss than separation from the love and fellowship of the Father. We were created with a wonderful desire for love and intimacy with others, but most especially with God through His Son and the Holy Spirit. Jesus gave us the greatest gift of all when He made it His priority to pay whatever price was necessary to reconcile us with the Father. The full pain of this price is unimaginable.

We shall never have to know such separation. All God asks is, "How shall we escape if we ignore such a great salvation?" (Hebrews 2:3). In other words, considering what Jesus went through to save the lost, and considering the horror of eternal separation from God, do we have any justification for sitting by passively and not sharing this wonderful Good News with others? He is not asking us to pay the price; it is finished. He is merely asking us to tell others what has already been purchased in *their* behalf.

And so we reach out to them. Why? Because it is a priority. Because God deserves all honor and glory. Because it brings God joy. Because it was Jesus' priority. But, always, because of His love.

3

THE MANDATE

Several years ago, a well-known evangelist was holding a crusade in Haiti. After the week-long crusade, some pastors from a remote village in the inland part of the island approached the evangelist and asked if he would be willing to come to their village to hold a series of meetings. They explained that many of their people could not attend the city crusade. After prayer, the evangelist consented to preach in the distant village.

The next day, they were driving up the winding, dirt road when the evangelist saw a small Coke stand by the road. Being thirsty from the Caribbean heat, he asked the pastor if they could stop and have a Coke. As they purchased their drinks, the evangelist felt compelled to share the Gospel with the young man behind the stand. He asked him if he knew Jesus. The young man replied, "Is that another American soft drink?"

Think about it. You can buy a Coke virtually anywhere around the world, and yet there are people who have yet to hear the name of Jesus. Some hours after Princess Diana died in a car accident, the whole world knew. Yet two thousand years after the King of kings died for the sins of the world, billions have yet to hear.

The mandate to reach the lost and perishing with the Good News of salvation is biblical: The Lord told His followers to be His witnesses upon this earth. This is, of course, as we have learned, the Great Commission. In fact, each of the four gospels ends with this evangelistic mandate from Jesus:

Then Jesus came to them and said, "All authority in heaven and on earth has been given to me. Therefore go and make disciples of all nations, baptizing them in the name of the Father and of the Son and of the Holy Spirit, and teaching them to obey everything I have commanded you. And surely I am with you always, to the very end of the age."

Matthew 28:18–20

He said to them, "Go into all the world and preach the good news to all creation."

Mark 16:15

"And repentance and forgiveness of sins will be preached in his name to all nations, beginning at Jerusalem."

Luke 24:47

Again Jesus said, "Peace be with you! As the Father has sent me, I am sending you."

John 20:21

We know what the Father sent Jesus to do: Preach the Gospel, heal the sick, cast out demons, raise the dead, bind up the brokenhearted, set the captives free and more (see

Luke 4:17–21). Not only did Jesus turn around and ask the disciples to do the same, but He also gave the authority and power to do it: "You will receive power when the Holy Spirit comes on you; and you will be my witnesses in Jerusalem, and in all Judea and Samaria, and to the ends of the earth" (Acts 1:8).

According to Church history and tradition, the early Church took this mandate seriously. The fruitful outcome of each apostle's life and the fact that many ended up giving their lives for the Gospel make the picture very clear. Well-respected tradition tells us that Peter took the Gospel to Asia Minor, to the Jews who remained in Babylon and in time to Rome—where he was crucified. Andrew established Christianity among the barbarian people of Scythia. Thomas preached and planted the Church among the stubborn Parthians. Eventually he founded Christianity in South India. Matthew proclaimed Christ in Anthropophagi, a land of cannibals, where he was executed—but the king's heart was moved as Matthew died; the king became a priest and led a movement of his own people into the faith. Tradition tells us that Philip was one of the great apostles of Asia, establishing Christianity in Athens and in Hierapolis, where he was executed. Simon the Zealot and Jude formed an apostolic team and communicated Christianity in Persia. James, the brother of John, was the apostle to Spain, where his body is buried. Bartholomew took Matthew's written gospel to India and preached there; he also became the apostle to Armenia (George G. Hunter III, *How to Reach Secular People*, Abingdon, 1992).

The Only Hope for a Dying World

Why did Jesus give us this mandate? Because in this temporal world, He is the only hope. The government is not the answer; education is not the answer; politics is not the answer; money or humanism is not the answer. There is only one answer and it is the Son of God. Yet vast numbers of people are dying and going to hell without this knowledge. Look at these figures. Out of the more than six billion people in the world today, three and a half billion have never heard the Gospel. Of these lost souls, more than one billion are Muslims and another billion are in China. About 1.3 billion persons worldwide have a Christian background, but are lost.

In comparison, 900 million individuals worldwide are born-again Christians. With no guilt or condemnation intended, I point out the simple reality that unless we evangelize the lost, vast numbers of people will perish.

Salvation does not reap only eternal rewards; God blesses His followers in this life as well. Where the Gospel has gone, it has also redeemed people from poverty and ignorance and brought transformation to society. I remember hearing Pat Robertson tell about a trip to India, during which he visited a village that was particularly poor. One home, however, stood out. It had electricity; it even had a refrigerator. It was not the mayor's home or a high official's home, but the home of a Christian man in a pagan land. He was prospering in the midst of squalor because he had received the Gospel—and the changes in his spiritual life touched his physical realm as well.

This is not a singular phenomenon. It is fact, for instance, that South Korea has prospered because of the Gospel—this is especially noticeable when you consider its neighbors. In the study of missions this is called "redemption and lift." That is because people are not only saved but also lifted out of poverty. Even the land is healed when the Gospel goes forth. In *Healing the Land*, Winkie Pratney describes how the places where the Gospel has spread enjoy flourishing vegetation. Where Islam has spread, conversely, the land has died.

A woman who works on my staff recalls her shock at what she saw on a short-term mission trip to the Dominican Republic. As the plane began its descent, both the Dominican Republic and Haiti, two island nations, came into view. Haiti looked lifeless—brown, fruitless and dismal. In contrast, lush tropical foliage and massive stands of banana trees crowded the borders and interior of the Dominican. It is interesting to note that the Haitian government—that very year—had declared voodoo its national religion.

It is accepted as the norm around the world that Christians—more than adherents of any other religion—establish the finest hospitals, schools and social services. With the King of the universe as our source, architect and motivator, we should expect the Gospel message to transform not only hearts but society as well. We live in a world with great needs that cannot be met by the systems or the best efforts of men. Truly the Gospel is the only hope for a dying world.

One Lifetime to Give

When you think about it, we will have matchless opportunities in heaven to continue enjoying the privileges of knowing God in even greater measure. We will enjoy unparalleled worship, unrestrained intimacy with Him, unfathomable depth of relationship with Jesus and our fellow believers, endless growth and discovery of the Kingdom, the delight of His continuous presence and so much more. Yet there is one thing that we will *never again* have the opportunity to do: We will never again have the opportunity to share Jesus Christ with the lost. What an incomprehensible thought!

I am first to covet worship time and being intimate with the Lord on this earth. As I shared in the first chapter, it is the ultimate priority. In heaven, it will never end. And regarding the attendant command to love others as ourselves, let me say that I enjoy fellowship as much as anyone. I get excited about the fact that we will have eternity to talk! And as far as growing and learning more about our great God, I am first in line at conferences and such to be equipped by the incredible ministers God has given to the Body of Christ. Can you fathom sitting under the teachings of the Church "greats"—much less Jesus Christ Himself—for all time? I am looking forward to the adventure of being able to learn forever—and even have every pesky doctrinal question answered. We will have all of these privileges forever. *But once we die, our chances to reach the lost are over.* This is not to minimize any Kingdom virtue, but to emphasize the urgency and the mandate of evangelism.

Years ago I had a chance to talk with the late Dr. Bill Bright in his hotel room. He founded Campus Crusade for Christ, the world's largest Christian ministry. He also wrote the *Four Spiritual Laws* tract and produced the *JESUS* film. His ministry led countless people to the Lord and trained multitudes of others to do the same.

I asked him how he had maintained his passion for the Lord. His answer was simple. "I believe that when we give ourselves to evangelism, we stay on the edge of spiritual vitality. I have always shared the Gospel with the lost. When I am with a non-Christian for more than thirty minutes, I see it as a divine appointment, and I know that I am to share the Gospel with that person. That is how I have maintained a passion for Jesus."

With this perspective it is hard to see how anyone can grow and become Christlike without consistently sharing his or her faith. I do not give you Dr. Bright's comments to make you feel obligated to lead your seatmate to the Lord on your next plane trip longer than thirty minutes. Granted, we do need to be aware of and take advantage of opportunities to share. But the point is that when we give ourselves to the ministry of evangelizing, the Lord gives us back more of Himself. After all, the Bible says that if we want to find life, we must give our lives away. Jesus said, "Whoever wants to save his life will lose it, but whoever loses his life for me will find it" (Matthew 16:25).

You might say that it is like the difference between the Dead Sea and the Sea of Galilee. The Jordan River flows into the Dead Sea, but it has no outlet. That great sea does not give out anything of itself; subsequently, nothing in it can survive. The Jordan River also flows into the Sea of Galilee—but it flows out. That sea by contrast has an abundance of life. When we "empty out our seas"—that is, give away the life within us for Jesus—we benefit tremendously.

This same principle that applies to the individual also applies to the local church. When a church is evangelizing and giving herself to reach the lost, the Lord will bless that church and give back to her with many kinds of increases. It reminds me of a nursery in the hospital. The happiest place is where the babies are. Churches that see souls saved on a regular basis enjoy a unique happiness and spiritual vitality that is contagious. There is nothing more fulfilling or life-infusing than leading a person to the Lord.

God in His goodness has given us a mandate that brings us great joy. Our ultimate fulfillment comes when we are conformed to the image of Jesus and are true worshipers of the Father. Jesus did this by laying down His life to bring others to the Father and to salvation. We will find our greatest satisfaction in life in doing the same.

SECTION 2

OUR PRESENTATION

4

YOUR LIFE
IS A WITNESS

Whether we realize it or not, our lives are our presentation of the Gospel—our presence is our witness. We might have very charismatic speaking abilities or unusual manifestations of the power gifts of the Holy Spirit. Yet if we have no character or integrity to go with them, our words and ministries have little lasting substance.

I once heard a true story about a Christian pastor who was put into prison because of his faith. He was placed into a cell that was already occupied by a hardened criminal, a murderer. As the days went by, the pastor tried to reach out to the man but with no success. The felon would simply respond by saying that he did not believe in God. The pastor loved him all the more.

One day as the pastor was sharing his faith he had a word of wisdom for his cellmate. He asked, "Do you want to know who Jesus is like?"

The murderer responded, "Yes."

The pastor said, "Jesus is like me."

The murderer thought for a while and then said, "If Jesus is like you, then I want to receive Jesus into my heart." He became a Christian.

As I heard that story, I had to ask myself how many non-Christian friends I could approach and say, "Jesus is like me," and find them wanting to be saved.

Think about the ramifications. We are here to represent Jesus to a dying and lost world. Jesus could send angels to the world to share the Gospel message. He could write the message in the sky. He could devise any number of methods for sharing the truth of His love. The method He has chosen, though, is to have His followers demonstrate and declare His Good News of salvation. This is what it means to be a witness for the Lord.

The truth of the matter is, we are witnesses either for or against Christ depending on our character. In *Youth Aflame* (Communication Foundation, 1970), Winkie Pratney writes:

> You do not have to learn to be a witness. You already ARE a witness! . . . You are telling the world right now what god you really belong to. . . . Your words and your life are tied inseparably together; you will always convey to others around you what you really love and live for most. . . . Anyone who watches you closely . . . can tell if you really mean what you claim with your lips.
>
> . . . What are YOU witnessing to? Your witness is the total package of your attitudes, character and actions. . . . No careful observer is fooled. . . . Whatever your god is, will show. . . . If it is anything else but Jesus, your closest friends already know. It will be the thing you like to talk most about, read most about, center your life around. . . . Could you get to heaven on the testimony of your next-door neighbor?
>
> If you have claimed to belong to [Jesus] but your life does not back up your words, men and women have re-

jected Christ and the Gospel because of you. That is why Jesus said, "He that is not for Me is against Me; and he that gathers not with Me scatters abroad."

I know of no Bible plan that will enable you to present Christ to others without your OWN life being Christ-like. True Christianity IS Christ! You can present another philosophy or religion without its founder by a "canned" plan, and change a few words to sell soap just as effectively with it; but you cannot present Christ to another until you properly represent Him and His love.

Think about how important character was in establishing the credibility of the New Testament Church. The actions, reactions and lifestyles of the early believers had incredible weight in determining the authenticity and the history of Christianity.

Lifestyle Evangelism

What is your life declaring? I like the term *lifestyle evangelism* because it connotes wholeness in communicating Christ. It means that our lives are a message. Often we think of evangelism as something we go and do on Saturday mornings with a group from church rather than something we live. Your character is who you really are, every day. When people see you, do they think of "good news" walking around? Is there enough of a smile on your face or joy in your life for someone else to want what you have? Certainly you do not have to be perfect, and there is nothing wrong with being honest about having a bad day, but, overall, what message are you sending about the success and enjoyment of your life?

Then there is the practical outworking of character and integrity found in what you do. What kinds of movie theaters or clubs do people find you walking out of? Are your bills paid? Are your finances in order and are you honest with your income taxes? How about when no one is watching: If the waitress makes a mistake with your check (in your favor) would you point it out to her? Do you have integrity that others recognize?

A friend told me a true story of an evangelist who was holding an evangelistic crusade in California. During the daytime, he wanted to do some sightseeing. At one point he stepped onto a bus and paid the fee, but discovered when he sat down that the bus driver had given him too much change. When the evangelist saw the extra money, he hesitated at first about whether or not he should give it back because it was only a small amount. Yet he knew better.

As he was getting off the bus, he said to the bus driver, "When I got on, you gave me too much change."

The bus driver replied, "I know. I did it on purpose. I was at your crusade last night and I wanted to see if you practice what you preach."

Think now. In everyday life, are you diligent in the details or do you do the least required of you just to "get by"? Are you the last to arrive at work and the first to leave? Do you keep commitments with your children? Is your yes, yes, and your no, no? Are you always late for appointments? Do you keep your word?

Some might question this kind of inventory: "Do these things really make a difference if I am out there sharing Christ?" Absolutely! Let me ask you a few more questions.

Are your relationships in order? Is your marriage healthy? Are you accountable to anyone for your spiritual growth? Are you stubborn when being entreated? Are you easily taught?

While you may be able to fool others in these matters, or even fool yourself, eventually you will be found out. The Lord does not delight in having His name shamed. We are not representing an encyclopedia company (though we should do that with integrity, too) but the Most High God.

According to the Word, God is not interested in our feats of accomplishment for Him but rather our relationship with Him. Anyone who maintains a close relationship with God knows how heartbreaking it is to displease Him and fall short of that which He intends. I believe one way you can gauge a person's true depth of intimacy with God is to take a look at his or her character. Anyone who is truly pursuing intimacy with the Lord could not handle the distance created by the gap in character for long. Take a look at this verse:

> "Not everyone who says to Me, 'Lord, Lord,' shall enter the kingdom of heaven, but he who does the will of My Father in heaven. Many will say to Me in that day, 'Lord, Lord, have we not prophesied in Your name, cast out demons in Your name, and done many wonders in Your name?' And then I will declare to them, 'I never knew you; depart from Me, you who practice lawlessness!'"
>
> Matthew 7:21–23, NKJV

Unlike humanistic reasoning and society's more-is-always-better mentality, the Lord is more concerned with relationship and character than He is with the lesser things we too often value. The world has become skeptical of many Christians and their organizations, and some for good reason: How tragic when the world's mindset permeates believers' lives, and headlines broadcast the huge deficits of character and integrity! Jesus is returning for a spotless Bride.

Being an Effective Witness

I remember hearing the late Derek Prince, scholar and Bible teacher, make a comment about methods of presenting the Gospel. He said that Christians should be like fine perfume. He told why: "Cheap perfume comes on strong and heavy.

Sometimes it is overwhelming. But fine perfume doesn't come on strong. Instead, the scent lasts and lingers even after the person wearing the perfume has left the room."

How many of us have been like cheap perfume, coming on strong and overwhelming the non-Christian? No wonder so many people have been turned off by our "witless witness"! I can tell you this because I used to shove the Gospel down people's throats. There was a period in my life when I drove up and down Georgia Avenue in Maryland looking for hitchhikers. I loved hitchhikers because once they were inside my car, they were trapped and had to listen to my evangelistic spiel!

God taught me about this zealous approach through my sister, Chung-Hae. Chung-Hae and I were very close as we grew up in America. The year I was converted, my sister was away at college. I could not wait until she came home for the summer so I could share the Gospel with her.

All that summer I tormented her with my preaching. Every opportunity I had, I forced the Gospel on Chung-Hae, thinking I was somehow blessing her. One day, after I had made her feel particularly guilty about not following Jesus, she looked me in the eye in a fit of rage and said, "Will you just shut up! I'm tired of your preaching. I'm tired of your making me feel bad for not following Jesus. Don't preach to me again."

I felt like saying, "Well, excuuuse me!" At the same time, I was convicted, stunned and terribly sorry for blowing it. I went to my room and had this conversation with the Lord: "Should I stop preaching and telling my sister about You, Lord? After all, we are told to share the Gospel regardless of persecution."

I sensed the Lord saying to me, *You're not being persecuted for righteousness' sake, but for your stupidity. Stop preaching and love her. Show her that I have changed your life.*

That was the last time I preached to her. A few weeks later Chung-Hae was alone in the house. She was doing her chores when the Spirit of the Lord started gently to draw her. As she was folding the laundry, she began to pray and ask God for forgiveness of her sins. Then she surrendered her heart to Jesus.

Later that day, she came up to me with a glow on her face and told me she had given her life to Jesus. Then she asked me, "Do you know what the turning point was?" I shook my head. She said, "When I saw you doing the dishes for Mom and taking out the trash, I knew something had happened to you."

I learned many invaluable things that day. I learned that my life is my message. I learned that people are watching. I did not take out the trash to impress my family members. I took it out because I was such a partying vagrant before I gave my life to the Lord that I hardly did anything constructive. After my conversion, I sincerely wanted to help and serve my mother.

Simply put, is your life a steppingstone for the Gospel or a stumbling block? Are you a witness for or against Christ by the character and integrity you reveal? What Gospel does your life preach to someone who may never set foot in a church?

I will share in the next chapter ways to undergird your character for more effective evangelism and a God-pleasing life.

5

BUILDING GODLY
CHARACTER

Character matters—especially when you are preaching the Gospel. And the foundation that I have found to be most vital to a solid structure of integrity is personal wholeness.

Let's begin with the story Jesus tells of two men who each built beautiful homes. One man built his home on a solid foundation; the other, on sand. When the storms raged (which they will in every one of our lives) the house built on sand collapsed, and the fall of that house was "great" (Matthew 7:27, NKJV).

This says to me that the destruction caused by the fall harmed more than just the house, which represented this man and his ministry. The fall of the house also had an impact on everyone who depended on that house. What you do with your life, especially if you desire to influence others for Jesus Christ, has far-reaching implications in the lives of others. That is why it is especially important for your foundation to be firmly laid on the rock of Jesus Christ. You simply cannot afford ruin.

We know we want godly character, but we do not always know how to get it. While there are many things people can impart to us through the "laying on of hands," such as certain gifts of the Spirit, character is not one of them. Can you imagine the altar call if that were possible? But you and I both know that it does not work that way.

On the one hand, God is at work in us—constantly conforming us into the image of Jesus. This is a sovereign work of God's grace. On the other hand, as sons and daughters we must cooperate willingly with God and His processes, growing and learning to develop godly character. We can do so quickly and obediently and save ourselves and others much pain (see Proverbs 10:1), or we can be like the mule, pulled along reluctantly by the bridle (see Psalm 32:9). It is our choice.

It is not enough to have the desire: We have to work hard on the execution. Just watching a professional athlete play his sport does not make you one. The athlete spends unseen hours preparing himself for the game. He trains his body severely and develops every mental aspect conducive to quick and sure responses. He lives his life for the sport; it is no weekend hobby. Likewise, if you do not give your all in the pursuit of character, you cannot expect it to be there when you need it. Christianity needs to be more than a weekend hobby.

Here are some practical principles and disciplines that can help us develop and exhibit character.

Maintain a Positive Attitude

Character is developed in the crucible of trials. How we respond to the difficulties life throws our way determines the degree to which we will be like Jesus. That is why Paul says confidently,

> We also rejoice in our sufferings, because we know that suffering produces perseverance; perseverance, character; and character, hope. And hope does not disappoint us, because God has poured out his love into our hearts by the Holy Spirit, whom he has given us.
>
> Romans 5:3–5

James concurs:

> Consider it pure joy, my brothers, whenever you face trials of many kinds, because you know that the testing of your faith develops perseverance. Perseverance must finish its work so that you may be mature and complete, not lacking anything.
>
> James 1:2–4

The writer of Hebrews admonishes believers with these words:

> And you have forgotten that word of encouragement that addresses you as sons: "My son, do not make light of the Lord's discipline, and do not lose heart when he rebukes you, because the Lord disciplines those he loves, and he punishes everyone he accepts as a son."
>
> Hebrews 12:5–6

I find these verses incredible: The things that cause worldly people to fall apart are the very things God *chooses* for us to further our stability! Imagine: The road to character is actually *built* from suffering and perseverance. True sonship is proved by being rebuked and disciplined. If you want to lack nothing in your character and disposition, accept every opportunity you are given to persevere. Every success is another notch in your belt.

These verses have encouraged me over the years, especially in two of the most difficult years of my life, 1989 and 1993. Compared with the tragedies others experience, my trials in those years may seem minor. But in my world, they were heart deaths of my life's vision.

In 1989, I had to die to a vision concerning world missions. This was an executive decision issued to me from our association of churches. As a result of the death of this vision—what I, in fact, considered my life's call—and the change in the group's philosophy of missions, many members left my local church. Seeing so many wonderful friends leave and having my direction in ministry change so drastically was extremely painful.

The second death of a vision took place in 1993 when the Lord led me to step down as senior pastor of the church that I had founded years before. God eventually led me to leave that church and its movement of which I had been part for more than eighteen years. The death of vision, dreams and relationships with the resulting questions, backlash and uncertainty was very painful.

Although the trials were difficult for my family and me, I genuinely thank God for them because I grew in greater dependence on the Lord alone—and in character. I have no regrets. I strove to maintain an attitude of blessing and to walk in love during each painful episode, leaving no open door as best I could so the enemy could not bring division or wounding through me to the Body of Christ. I overrode my feelings so that I could display a Christlike attitude and continue sharing His nature in the midst of circumstances.

Maintaining the right attitude in the middle of suffering and difficulties yields true victory and maturity. Our decisions about our attitudes in each trial we face will cause us either to graduate to the next level of godliness or to have to repeat the test under different circumstances. Remember how the Israelites grumbled and complained in the wilderness? Instead of entering into the Promised Land, they had to wander around the wilderness for another forty years. If you want to move on with God, maintaining the right attitude is crucial in developing godly character.

Be Filled Anew with the Holy Spirit

We will study this in more depth in chapter 12, "The Holy Spirit's Mission," but we can note for now that we need His filling in order to have Christ's power in our lives. This filling is what gives us the ability to walk like Jesus and turn away from all of our fleshly or lower desires. We are called to be like Him, and it takes His very nature controlling us in order to do this. This is how we have Christ's character.

This filling is not a one-time event. We require regular or continual infilling of the Spirit. Many of the disciplines of the Christian life help fill me anew, but the three that have the most impact come from my intimate love relationship with Jesus. These "big three" are worship, prayer and meditating on God's Word. These are my uncompromised "dailies."

Worship

Worship is our hearts' ultimate expression of love for the Father. It helps us fulfill the Great Commandment like nothing else. You will recall that God created us to worship Him.

But something else takes place during worship that helps us in our goal of building a life of integrity: The Bible tells us that we eventually become what we continually behold (see 2 Corinthians 3:18). Thus, when we worship Jesus, we become more like Jesus. When we worship Him, we see Him as He is. Nothing else can give us the same revelation. Many times when I worship, His presence literally overtakes me. Then when I share the Gospel with others, He shines through.

If we want to have the character of Christ, we must behold Him. When we truly know of whom we speak, we can more readily give Him away.

Prayer

"Prayer—secret, fervent, believing prayer—lies at the root of all personal godliness," penned William Carey, the father of the modern missionary movement. We might think that the result of prayer is to "move God," but renowned Christians of all ages cite prayer as the one thing that most often *changes them.*

Richard Foster, author of the bestselling *Celebration of Discipline* (Harper & Row, 1978), offers similar insight:

> To pray is to change. Prayer is the central avenue God uses to transform *us.* If we are unwilling to change, we will abandon prayer as a noticeable characteristic of our lives. The closer we come to the heartbeat of God the more we see our need and the more we desire to be conformed to Christ.

Prayer allows God time to speak to us and lovingly lead us. If we will listen, He can use our time in prayer to guide our steps and to deliver us from wrong thinking, wrong habits and wrong desires. He will melt our hearts to fall more in love with Him. I find that as He does this, I desire to do more of what He is asking—not because I have to but because I want to.

Gone are my days of coming to God with my "laundry list" of requests. Granted, there are always times when I have fervent needs and people of many nations on my heart, and I do present them to my Father. But I want to hear what He is looking for first. My Abba knows what is on my heart, but sometimes He would rather speak His words of love to me.

Knowing His heart is part of how prayer changes us. According to Foster's further insight:

"You ask and do not receive, because you ask wrongly, to spend it on your passions" (James 4:3). To ask "rightly" involves transformed passions, total renewal. In prayer, real prayer, we begin to think God's thoughts after Him: to desire the things He desires, to love the things He loves. Progressively we are taught to see things from His point of view.

By seeing from God's point of view, we are far more likely to ask in prayer the things that are His will. The Bible promises we will receive them. This makes far more sense than praying from our own desires.

And by listening in prayer, the Holy Spirit guides us and directs not only our prayers but also our lives. More and more, we are led by the Spirit. Less and less, we give in to the flesh. We find ourselves becoming and praying like Jesus. We begin to do what we see the Father doing. We are more united with the Father and moving in His love and power simply by being changed in His presence through prayer (see John 17:20–24).

Meditating on the Word

When I was a young Christian, I was terribly carnal. I was angry, for starters. Then I heard a man of God say that if you want to overcome your carnality and become more Christlike in character, meditate on God's Word.

I repented of my anger and began to memorize every key verse in the Bible concerning anger. As I did that, God delivered me from my angry heart. Ask my wife!

When I saw in me the ugly sin of pride and selfish ambition, I memorized all the key verses concerning pride and humility. When I struggled with lust, I memorized Romans 6 and other relevant verses. In fact, there were so many flaws in my character, I ended up memorizing more than 55 chapters in the Bible. While I could not quote every verse of these chapters to you today, I can tell you that every one of those life-giving Scriptures of truth sank into my spirit and transformed my life.

Just as the Word says, "How can a young man keep his way pure? By living according to your word" (Psalm 119:9). By constantly meditating or "chewing" on the Word of God (which literally means the way a cow chews the cud), our character is changed.

Practicing these spiritual disciplines not only cultivates the most awesome relationship we could ever have—that with our Lord and Savior Jesus Christ—but also, by helping us be filled anew, it builds our character into His image.

Be Committed to the Local Church

One of the quickest ways to find out how mature you are in character is to have it "rubbed" by someone in the local church. The local church is like an extended family where all learn and grow together. That means learning to love each other, warts and all.

The Bible lists more than fifty "one another" verses such as "love one another," "serve one another," "admonish one another," "encourage one another." As we actually do these things, we mature and develop in character and wholeness. This is hard to do if you are sitting at home alone watching Christian television. Coming to an occasional get-together is not the essence of Christian community. "As iron sharpens iron, so one man sharpens another" (Proverbs 27:17).

Through relationship, discipleship, accountability, service, worship and many other benefits that the local church provides, one grows in maturity and Christlikeness. And by interacting with people different from ourselves, we learn to love and appreciate uniqueness. We can further experience the delight of seeing in them different aspects of the Lord Himself, which we might never have known without the honor of having them in our lives.

Face Bitter Roots in Your Inner Man

For many years, I focused on developing character in every way I knew. I was diligent to be accountable to those in authority over me. I worked to improve quantifiable things in my life—such as daily Bible studies, being on time, learning how to be a better husband and parent, financial responsibility and so forth. Yet there were areas where I could not seem to gain the victory no matter how hard I tried. One of those areas was my marriage to Sue.

During all the years I worked on character development, I never heard about heart wounds or bitter-root sin patterns, or how these unhealed areas keep us from emotional freedom. I was striving to spend quality time with Sue, but I was actually treating her badly in other ways because of unforgiveness I had toward my father. (My book *Into the Fire* gives a more complete explanation of the difficulties and healing process.)

Let me explain. For years, I had judged my father for rejecting me. I forgave him when I first became a Christian, but I did not realize how I had continued to judge him—and my mother, too.

God's maxim on this subject is clear: "Judge not, that you be not judged" (Matthew 7:1, NKJV). When you judge others, you end up reaping what you have sown. Because I had judged my parents, I reaped judgment in my life: I actually did the same thing. I rejected the people closest to me—especially my wife. As a result, our marriage was not healthy for many years.

When God graciously began to reveal this root issue through the teaching of John and Paula Sandford, I was able to repent of the judgment toward my parents. Immediately the spirit and the curse of rejection were broken off of my life. It completely changed my interaction with Sue and many others. I asked her forgiveness. Our marriage was revolutionized. Greater love and acceptance were released in my life, not only toward her but toward others as well—including myself. (Yes, you can judge and reject yourself, and have a bitter root grow from it.)

You can see how the lack of such freedom could affect my relationships with so many people—especially if I thought they were rejecting me. And when you are witnessing to people, many times they *are* rejecting you. If you are wounded, your response may be anything but godly. If you are very wounded, your pain may keep you from witnessing in the first place. But you can be set free and move into personal wholeness.

Take a little self-inventory. Consider the possibility of underlying bitter roots or wounding if you find yourself doing any of the following: Reacting to someone far out of proportion to what he or she has said or done; feeling angry or shutting yourself down without knowing why; always feeling rejected; treating a particular person or particular culture with prejudice and mocking. These are just a few examples. Most of us are fully willing to take a look at surface things, but many times we have no understanding of their deeper import.

Many people think that once they become Christians, everything is made new in Christ and they never have to deal with things from the past. If this is your view, I must tell you from painful years of experience that I have not found this to be true. Just as we are immediately justified when we are saved, but progressively sanctified as we live out our salvation, so I believe that there is progression when it comes to our inner man. God says in His Word that He desires truth in our innermost being (see Psalm 51:6). That should be a goal of character development and personal wholeness, and it often takes prayer and work to accomplish it.

The Bible also says that we must lay the ax at the *root* of a problem (see Matthew 3:10). If we just chop off the top branches of a tree, for instance, it will continue to grow; we have done nothing to damage the life-giving root.

Sue and I had a tree in our front yard next to the driveway where we parked our car. Not only did the sap from the tree drip onto the car, but the birds resting on the branches did "their thing" on it as well. The final straw was when the tree's root system began to break up the driveway. Finally we decided to have the tree chopped down, but we could not stop there. We had to dig up the stump and kill the roots or the system would continue to grow and damage the driveway. Similarly we may apologize for our hurtful actions, but until we deal with the roots of anger or fear or mistrust, they will grow as strongly as ever and damage whatever they come into contact with.

If there are recurring sins in your life that you cannot seem to master through prayer and the Word, ask the Holy Spirit to reveal any root issue(s) that may be causing those sins or attitudes. Once the roots are discovered and repentance spoken, you will experience a new level of holiness and freedom. I highly recommend the resources of both the Elijah House Ministry of John and Paula Sandford, based in Spokane, Washington, and Chester and Betsy Kylstra's Healing House, based in Santa Rosa Beach, Florida, to help you to address any sinful roots or patterns in your life.

Seek Deliverance

Just as many Christians do not believe they have to deal with their attitudes or wounds from the past, many also believe they never have a need for deliverance. I have found this, as well, not to be so. My purpose in this book is not to debate the topic of whether or not a Christian can have a demon. To help you in your quest to evangelize, I would simply like to state that I believe Christians most certainly can be tormented by demons. Perhaps they have been with you for so many years you actually think they are just part of your personality (this is known as a familiar spirit). Perhaps you were a missionary in a foreign country and picked up a spirit of infirmity or fear.

Whatever the source and whatever the boundaries of torment, I urge you to ask other Christians with authority to pray for you if you feel there is an area in your life where you are overtly troubled and cannot get free. If you have dealt with any bitter roots or sins that the Lord has revealed and yet still have no victory in an area, it is definitely time to consider the possibility that a demon is attacking you. We do not war with flesh and blood, but against powers and principalities (see Ephesians 6:12). This is not a matter of shame but reality. We are spiritual beings living a temporary human existence, not human beings living a temporary spiritual life. We are learning to live in the unseen realm and discovering that what is unseen is more real and eternal than what is seen. Please do not neglect deliverance or its place in your journey for character and wholeness.

Keep Your Eye on the Vision

Keeping my eye on God's vision for my life keeps me focused on the race. When I think of the end-time call for the harvest and how God has chosen me for this very hour, my heart beats faster. I am like a racehorse readied at the starting gate. All else fades from view as I see the Master bid me to His call. This vision helps me say no to sin because I do not want to jeopardize my future over some cheap thrill today.

I believe you are reading this book because you are just as committed to the purposes of God. His vision is just as vital. If it is not yet clear to you, God will make it so. Ask Him in prayer, and seek the wise counsel of those He has placed in your life. Proverbs 29:18 (KJV) states that "where there is no [progressive] vision, the people perish"—or run fruitlessly in endless circles. I know that is not your destiny.

I find that keeping my eye on the vision keeps me on the cutting edge. I constantly cut away or say no to anything that does not further the goals God has for my life. Having a vision helps me to "beat my body and make it my slave" (1 Corinthians 9:27).

As I write this chapter, the summer Olympics are taking place. The physical and mental discipline of these athletes who are pursuing the vision of an Olympic medal should embarrass many Christians—including me. Why? Because their incredible hourly, daily, sometimes lifelong sacrificial commitment for something that will one day perish makes my commitment pale in comparison. My vision is for something eternal. Should I not work to build my character in every way possible? Is service through personal wholeness not worth every effort?

Look at these thought-provoking words spoken by a man who was dedicated to the vision of spreading Communism around the world. These words were recorded in Michael Green's book *Evangelism through the Local Church* (Nelson, 1992):

> We communists have a high casualty rate. We are the ones who get shot and hung and lynched and jailed, slandered and ridiculed and fired from our jobs, and in every other way made as uncomfortable as possible. A certain percentage of us get killed and imprisoned. We live in virtual poverty. . . . We have been described as fanatics. We are fanatics. Our lives are dominated by one great overshadowing factor—the struggle for world communism.

We communists have a philosophy of life, which no amount of money can buy. We have a cause to fight for, a definite purpose in life. We subordinate our petty personal selves into a great movement of humanity, and if our personal lives seem hard, we are adequately compensated by the thought that each of us, in his small way, is contributing to something new and true and better for mankind.

There is one thing in which I am in dead earnest, and this is the communist cause. It is my life, my business, my religion, my hobby, my wife, my mistress, my bread and meat. I work at it in the daytime and dream of it by night. Its hold on me grows, not lessens, as time goes by. Therefore I cannot carry on a friendship, a love affair, or even a conversation without relating it to this force which both drives me and guides my life. . . . I've been to jail because of my ideas, and if necessary I'm ready to go before a firing squad.

If people are willing to die for a temporal vision, how much more should we give ourselves to the eternal God and lover of our souls for His purposes?

Consider that thought as you labor in love and the power of the Holy Spirit to see your character become like Christ's and your inner man become whole. Then serve Him by evangelizing a world without those privileges and honors.

6

LOVING AND
ACCEPTING OTHERS

Years ago, I was invited to Indiana University to speak at an outreach meeting. I decided to walk around the campus and get a feeling for the university before I spoke that evening. As my pastor friend gave me a tour of the campus, we noticed an angry crowd of students screaming at a man who appeared to be preaching at them. As we drew closer we heard the preacher calling the female students "whores," "sluts" and other derogatory names. He was calling others "sodomites," "perverts" and "queers." No wonder the students were angry!

I had never witnessed anything like this before. Within me, a righteous anger arose toward that preacher. *This is not the gospel*, I said to myself, and decided to do something about it. I went up to the man and told him that I was a pastor visiting the university as a guest speaker. I asked if I could preach to the crowd. He graciously consented. I got up and shared my testimony. The crowd fell silent. I spoke on the love of God and the grace of God. Everything the other preacher did, I did the opposite. He screamed, ranted and raved. I spoke conversationally and did my best to convey God's love through my facial expression, tone of voice and gestures. In the end, I gave an invitation and six students gave their lives to Jesus.

When it comes to effective evangelism, there is no substitute for genuine Christlike love. God's love is the greatest force in the universe. It was His love that motivated God to give His only Son. It was His love that led Jesus to lay down His life for us even though we were sinners and enemies of God. It was His love that moved Paul to go to the Gentiles and compel them to be reconciled to God. And it is God's love shining through His people that will draw the lost to the Savior.

Jesus must be our example when it comes to evangelism. We can safely say that Jesus conquered the world through His love. The way that He spent time with the unlovely, the way that He affirmed the unlikely, the way that He encouraged the untouchable—all were ways that Jesus demonstrated His love.

This kind of love will truly win the lost. Fear is a great motivator, but fear does not bear fruit in keeping with God's Kingdom. Fire-and-brimstone preaching might scare someone into believing in Jesus, but that method does not really win hearts. Without a revelation of love, it is unlikely that a "fear convert" will easily or graciously evangelize others—except out of his or her own shaky fear motivation. As we said in the first chapter, lovers make the best servants. You do not burn out or quit when you are fueled by the fire of passion for Jesus. He was comfortable with all kinds of people, and He was rebuked for it. He was a friend of sinners and tax gatherers, and He was called names because of it. He talked to the "wrong kinds" of women, and He was judged on account of it. Yet He looked past man's reactions and loved freely in spite of it.

There are many ways to define God's love. I personally believe it is best demonstrated by two words: *commitment* and *acceptance*. *Commitment* means that love is not some nebulous feeling. Rather, love is a conscious choice of your will. Love is unselfish and works for the greatest good of others. It does not change daily, depending on whether you are up or down. Love has pure motives and is unconditional in its nature. If you treat me badly, I will not withdraw my love. If you are sick, lose your job or become disfigured, I do not change my mind about you.

That is commitment. There are no strings attached. It is not, "I love you because you love me" or "I'll give to you because you gave to me." It is a commitment, regardless. We cannot make this commitment to love and accept others in our own strength; Jesus willingly infuses us with His love when we ask and when we are filled with His Holy Spirit. Human nature has selfish motives for love. That is why God's love is so extraordinary, so healing and so wonderful.

If we would truly practice this love, it would revolutionize the Church. If we would take it beyond our four walls, it would change the world. We would accept people unconditionally. We would stand by them no matter what they were going through. We would think the best and not the worst; build them up and not tear them down. People would feel safe in our presence. They would feel safe enough to fail and still know that they are loved no matter how they look or act. They would never feel judged. The world and the Church are desperate for this kind of love. It is never misinterpreted as a license to sin; rather, it means loving people for who they are just as Christ loves His Church.

Love is also demonstrated through *acceptance*. Acceptance is the opposite of rejection. The world is full of rejected people—some more obvious than others. Shortly after my conversion, I attended an outdoor performance. A nearby concession stand was selling food and drinks, so I walked over to buy something. The lines were long—except one. At the end of that short line stood a girl, and no one lined up behind her. Why? She was physically deformed, looking something like the Elephant Man. You could pick up the rejection and the pain she felt. I intentionally stood behind her to show my love. I wanted to hold her and say there is a God who loves you and cares for you. I learned that day how cruel the world can be.

It especially saddens me when Christians reject others. It could be rejection toward the street person, the homosexual, the drug addict, the prostitute or the biker. It could be toward a person of a different race or culture. I want to say emphatically that we cannot reach this world without demonstrating genuine acceptance.

Once again Jesus is our example. Whether it was the woman caught in adultery or the hated tax collector Zacchaeus or the prostitutes or drunkards, Jesus accepted and *interacted* with them all. It is one thing to make a mental assent that you accept people who are different from you. It is quite another to talk with those persons, to show your love through eye contact or a touch on the hand, to make them feel comfortable, to invite them into your home, to include them in conversation with your friends, to bring them along to an activity where you might otherwise be embarrassed to be seen with them. If anyone should feel comfortable with those who might be "unlovely" to the world, it should be the Christian, for we have the love of Christ to shore us up, to accept us unconditionally, to assure us when we feel awkward or unloved, to be there with open arms whenever we are unlovely, which we know we all are at times. What we freely receive, we freely give.

In *Out of the Salt Shaker* (InterVarsity, 1979) Rebecca Manley Pippert explains that to show love, we must also accept what people are willing to give us in return:

> In order to establish trust with people we must love them with the baggage they bring with them. We need to accept them where they are without compromising our Christian standards. Jesus accepted the "gift" from the prostitute at Simon's banquet (Luke 7:36–50). He shattered his "testimony" by allowing a loose woman to touch him. But he did not ask her to demonstrate her love for him and sense of forgiveness by exegeting Ezekiel. He allowed her to offer a gift that she was comfortable with.

The fact that Jesus demonstrated His love by accepting sinners does not mean He condoned their sins. Acceptance is different from approval. Rather, it means that He understood where they were coming from and accepted them for who they were. If we want to be effective in reaching the lost, we must demonstrate the quality of Christ's love as expressed in unconditional acceptance. After all, Jesus did that for you and me before we knew any better! You cannot expect an unbeliever to act like a believer until he or she is one.

On a practical level, here are some more tips:

- I began this chapter by telling about the offensive preacher on the college campus. He stands as an example of what we must never do. We must never demean or insult others or call them derogatory names. We must never come across as "more than" to their "less than." In humility, we share Christ. This does not mean we cannot be confident. After all, we are sharing Truth.
- As Scripture says, we must not be easily offended. Many people are wounded (often by Christians who

have "witnessed" to them) so we must be careful not to take their cynicism and distrust personally.

• Be willing to invest time. If you are able to spend time on more than one occasion sharing the Gospel with those who have never received it, you usually find that their walls will begin to break down and they will begin to trust you. In that environment, they are more likely to believe what you say, and your witness of Christ has greater entrance into their hearts. Time gives an expression of love and affirmation that cannot always be achieved by, say, handing out tracts and moving on. Please note that tracts are useful in many situations if shared with genuine caring. And, for that matter, many a soul has been saved by a one-time encounter with a Christian. (For a stunning story in this regard, see Appendix 4: "The Witness of One Little Man.") But generally people need to feel the affirmation that only time can give before they will listen to the Gospel message.

• Be open to doing things the "opposite way": You do not have to lead someone to Christ before he or she can come with you to a fellowship time or Bible study. Sometimes being involved in these activities is the very avenue God uses to open hearts to salvation. A young Chinese man showed up one day at a church I used to pastor. He was atheistic, suicidal and had terrible self-esteem. People in our congregation were wonderful. They welcomed him warmly in the services and other church events. I shared the Gospel with him many times, but he could not receive it. He did, however, ask a lot of questions, and every question was patiently answered. He continued to struggle, and people continued to love him unconditionally. After six months of attending services and receiving the love and acceptance of the people in the church, he finally gave his life to the Lord. Now he is a dynamic and beautiful Christian.

- Never consider an unbeliever as a "number" to be added to a quota. He or she is a precious son or daughter for whom Christ died. Treat unbelievers as you would your own brothers or sisters or mother—and love them to Christ. Do not compel them into words of acceptance when their hearts have not yet been won.

The Pharisees judged and rejected sinners. Jesus accepted and forgave sinners. If I asked which of the two you would like to emulate, you would no doubt say Jesus. I have found, however, that there is a Pharisee in all of us. It is good to examine our own hearts. I know that I have judged harshly and rejected those who were outside of the Church, as well as those in the Church. I have deeply repented of my pharisaic attitudes. I have made a commitment to love people under every circumstance, with no exception. I have promised God never to reject anyone—regardless of race, social status, education, background or any unique situation—and to accept everyone without reservation. Will you join me in this commitment of love and acceptance?

Together, as we choose to walk in God's love and acceptance, we will be about the Father's business and, like Jesus, we will do what we see the Father do. The results will be multiplied salvation of souls and gladdening of the Father's heart as His children come home.

SECTION 3

PRACTICAL
EVANGELISM

7

Know Your Message

Two days ago, a young Chinese man asked me what distinguishes Christianity from Buddhism. He told me that some Chinese people are not impressed with Christian witnessing through signs and wonders because Buddhist priests have also performed miracles and healing. And, like Christians, Buddhist priests teach their people to model love and kindness.

I responded that what separates Christianity from all other religions is our *message*. Even with extraordinary personal character or incredible power demonstrations of God, if we do not preach the Gospel we miss His primary way to evangelize the lost. The apostle Paul makes it clear:

"Everyone who calls on the name of the Lord will be saved." How, then, can they call on the one they have not believed in? And how can they believe in the one of whom they have not heard? And how can they hear without someone preaching to them? And how can they preach unless they are sent? As it is written, "How beautiful are the feet of those who bring good news!"

Romans 10:13–15

What is our message? Let's look at six essential truths of our evangelistic message. Then we will review the basics of how to start a conversation and share the Good News with an unbeliever.

The Six Essential Truths

1. The Gospel

The first truth of our evangelistic message is the Good News about Jesus Christ. In Corinthians, the apostle Paul defines the essence of the Gospel:

> Now, brothers, I want to remind you of the gospel I preached to you, which you received and on which you have taken your stand. By this gospel you are saved, if you hold firmly to the word I preached to you. Otherwise, you have believed in vain. For what I received I passed on to you as of first importance: that Christ died for our sins according to the Scriptures, that he was buried, that he was raised on the third day according to the Scriptures, and that he appeared to Peter, and then to the Twelve.

1 Corinthians 15:1–5

The Gospel message is the stunning story of what Jesus has done for us. It is a faithful recounting of how Jesus willingly took our places and died for our sins. It is testimony to the fact that He sacrificed His life on the cross to make us right with God in the only way possible as the only perfect sacrifice. It is the promise of the forgiveness of sins and the gift of eternal life to all who repent and believe.

When you tell this Good News to others, you are, as my good friend Pastor Bill Johnson says, actually "representing" Christ to the world. You present Him anew by your tone of voice, the love in your eyes, your caring words and other ways as you speak of the pearl of great price. In other words, the way you impart the message is also an essential part of the message.

Scanning the scene for other activities, answering your cell phone, acting rushed or inconvenienced while you talk about Christ certainly does not represent the Christ I know. Viewing the person you hope to reach as though there were no other person on earth, as though you had found your own lost son or daughter, is more like the loving Christ.

Even then, not everyone will receive this message. I heard, for instance, how a veteran returning from combat in Iraq listened to a preacher tell how Jesus had died for the sins of the world. After the service, he went up to the preacher and told him that he was not impressed with Jesus. He said, "I just came back from Fallujah. During combat, a buddy of mine jumped on a grenade to save me and our other friends—and he was no saint. What makes your Jesus so much better than my friend?"

The pastor wisely answered, "Your friend died for you and your friends, but he would have never died for a terrorist. The Bible says that while we were enemies of God, Jesus died for us. That is the difference between your friend and Jesus."

The reason why the Gospel made no sense to the veteran initially is because he did not really see himself as an enemy of God. He did not see his sins and how he had offended a holy God. Much of that has to do with spiritual warfare. As the Bible states, "The god of this age has blinded the minds of unbelievers, so that they cannot see the light of the gospel of the glory of Christ" (2 Corinthians 4:4). People often do not appreciate the Good News because we have neglected to express the second essential component of our message—the law.

2. The Law

When I talk about the law as truth and preaching the law, I am not saying that we have to obey or follow a certain set of rules in order to obtain salvation. Nor am I referring to Jewish ceremonial rules and regulations. I am talking about using the Scriptures to bring the knowledge and conviction of sin (see Romans 3:20).

Many people, especially in the United States, have no conviction of sin because they have no knowledge of the law. They go "with the flow" of pop culture or what is generally practiced in society; anything acceptable by man's standards is fine. They have no idea that their actions can offend the righteous Judge of their souls. When sinners are confronted by the law, they face (perhaps for the first time) a concrete definition of sin, the reality of judgment and the truth of a holy God. Most importantly, they are confronted with *their* sins and pierced in their hearts. They face a crucial challenge: They cannot free themselves; they must acknowledge their need for the help of God.

We know that the law offers no means of salvation, for we are saved by grace through faith alone (see Ephesians 2:8). Like the apostle Paul, however, we can make use of the law so "that every mouth may be stopped, and all the world may become guilty before God. . . . For by the law is the knowledge of sin" (Romans 3:19–20, NKJV).

Let me give you two practical illustrations of how the law brings individuals to see their sins and their need for God. I was open-air preaching at the University of North Carolina in Charlotte. After speaking, I mingled with the students who were interested or who had questions.

One particular student told me that he grew up in the church. He said that he had gone forward during an altar call and, therefore, was saved. Yet as I talked with him, I began to discern that either he was not a Christian or else he had backslidden. He rarely read the Bible, did not feel that he needed to be a part of a local church and did not see the importance of sharing the Gospel with others. In fact, he felt that one's faith was a private thing and should be kept between the individual and God. As I shared the importance of these spiritual disciplines, it became obvious that I was getting nowhere with him. So I asked him a question. The conversation went something like this:

"How is your moral life?"

"What do you mean?" he asked.

"Do you have a girlfriend?"

"Yes."

"Do you have a sexual relationship with her?"

"Yes," he acknowledged, but added quickly, "I believe having sex with your girlfriend is okay as long as you love the person."

I responded by opening my Bible to 1 Corinthians 6:9 and said, "You think you are a Christian and that you are going to heaven, but look at what the Bible says about fornication: Fornicators will not inherit the kingdom of God."

As soon as he saw the verse for himself, deep conviction came over him. I asked if he wanted to repent of his sins and get right with God. Unfortunately, he did not want to give up his sexual relationship with his girlfriend, so he walked away like the rich young ruler in the Bible—grieved.

Another time, a young man walked up to talk with me. He, too, thought he was a Christian because he had "raised his hand" to accept Christ at a church service. Now he was struggling with alcohol and fornication. In fact, he had gotten drunk every day before he made the decision to follow Christ, and he had gotten drunk every day since he had made the decision to follow Christ. Once again, I turned to that passage in Corinthians and showed him where the

81

Word says that drunkards and fornicators will not inherit the Kingdom of God.

He said to me, "You mean I am not saved?"

"According to this passage, you're not. The Good News is that you can be if you truly repent."

This young man humbly repented of his sins right on the spot and was instantly transformed and delivered of alcohol. Today he is a mature Christian with a wonderful family and leads a small group in his church. Once again, the law was used to bring knowledge and conviction of sin, and it changed this young man's life.

Many people do not like sharing the law because this is where many unbelievers will walk away from you. Yet no matter how difficult it is, sharing the truth in love *is* love because it offers the opportunity for true repentance that leads to eternal life—whether they respond to you or not. When you present the truth, a seed is sown. The hand of God can then nurture that seed, helping it grow into the conviction that may lead to future salvation.

The late Francis Schaeffer, Christian philosopher and author, is alleged to have said this: "If I had one hour with a truly secular person, I would spend the first fifty minutes sharing the law and then when he is thoroughly convinced how he has offended a holy God, I would spend the last ten minutes sharing the love and forgiveness of God found in Jesus Christ." While I might not give the Gospel message in quite the same way, I do agree with Schaeffer's principle that the law is a crucial part of sharing the truth effectively.

3. Repentance

The third truth of the evangelistic message is the need for repentance. More than seventy times the words *repent* or *repentance* appear in the New Testament. Jesus preached, "Repent, for the kingdom of heaven is near" (Matthew 4:17) and "I have not come to call the righteous, but sinners to repentance" (Luke 5:32).

Many people misunderstand the true nature of repentance. Repentance is not feeling sorry for your sins. The rich, young ruler, whom we mentioned above, felt sorrowful when Jesus told him how to obtain eternal life, and yet he walked away without changing his ways (see Matthew 19:21–22). Nor is repentance feeling convicted about your sins. Agrippa and Festus were convicted when they heard Paul preach, but as far as we know they never changed (see Acts 26). Repentance is not even confessing your sins. People confess their sins to their priests, pastors and counselors every day without changing.

Some define repentance as a complete reversal of direction. You were going one way; you turn around and go the other way. Others define it as completely changing your mind about something, and also your corresponding actions. When you repent you will, by God's grace, do whatever it takes at whatever it costs to change.

My definition is this: *Repentance* is God's gracious invitation to turn from selfish thinking and sin and turn one's heart to Him.

4. Faith

The fourth truth of the evangelistic message is the importance of faith. For me, saving faith is to believe in Jesus and what He has done, and to surrender our lives to Him. It is important to explain that this means letting go of our control and trusting in an unseen God. Faith is different from works, as we can never be saved by our works. This is an important distinctive in our message since well-intentioned people usually believe that their good works will give them access to heaven. Our message needs also to describe the unseen nature of faith, and yet express how faith is actual "substance" (Hebrews 11:1, NKJV).

5. Baptism in Water and with the Holy Spirit

The fifth truth of our message is the need for water baptism and the infilling of the Holy Spirit. The early Church obviously preached the importance of water baptism. The minute Philip's new Ethiopian convert spotted water from his chariot window, he practically jumped in in order to be baptized (see Acts 8:26–39). And Peter's message about the indwelling Holy Spirit was the norm of that day: "Repent and be baptized . . . in the name of Jesus Christ for the forgiveness of your sins. And you will receive the gift of the Holy Spirit" (Acts 2:38). If we consider the book of Acts as our model for the New Testament Church today, then both baptisms appear to be the standard for our experience.

I believe that we must return to a radical emphasis and practice of the doctrine of baptisms, because they are foundational for the believer's life (see Hebrews 6:1–2). Some churches and movements have allowed water baptism to slip to the "back burner" on the priority list. While this may not be intentional, I believe it is doing great harm. Water baptism confirms the death of the old man, the complete separation from old things and being raised as a new creature in Christ. And as you will see in the chapters that follow, baptism with the Holy Spirit confers His power upon the believer.

With these baptisms, a declaration is made both in the natural and spiritual realms that is unparalleled. I believe that this is crucial to a new believer's success, and essential for a victorious and fruitful Christian life.

6. Commitment to a Local Church

The final truth of our evangelistic message is one that I have stressed: commitment to a local church. I believe that having the privilege of leading someone to the Lord and not helping direct him or her to a solid local church is like taking a newborn baby from the delivery room and leaving him or her on the sidewalk. It is not a good start!

God's intent was for His family to grow, learn, be supported, edified, corrected and loved in a local church setting. The church is a place of godly relationships, transformation, service, safety, outreach, identity, fellowship and so much more. Without it, what began as a healthy seed will die for lack of nurture and godly care.

In this day and age, we simply cannot afford to be "lone rangers." Our society prizes an independent spirit, but that is no prize to God. He sees it as pride and selfishness, and the devil sees it as an open invitation to separate a sheep further from the fold. I do understand, of course, that some individuals cannot personally attend the activities of a local church because of physical or other restrictions. This is a golden opportunity for the church to go beyond her four walls and take the community of love to them.

How to Lead a Person to Christ

For many people, the most difficult part of sharing the Gospel is simply breaking the ice and gaining the other person's interest in having a conversation. I describe here a method that is simple to remember and works well. It is a basic way to initiate a conversation and lead a person to Christ.

I have taken this model from Jesus as He witnessed to the woman at the well, as told in John 4. He incorporated seven steps as He reached out to her. Here are those steps for our own use in evangelizing.

1. Initiate

Initiate the conversation. The Samaritan woman came to the well, and Jesus spoke to her: "Jesus said to her, 'Will you give me a drink?'" (John 4:7).

85

- Initiate conversation with the non-Christian. Asking a question is often a good way to start.
- Use the natural occasion to get the person's attention.

2. Interest

Draw the person's interest. This request for a drink was unusual, because Jews did not associate with Samaritans. She responded, "You are a Jew and I am a Samaritan woman. How can you ask me for a drink?" (John 4:9).

- Take a genuine interest in the person. Be loving and accepting.
- Be an excellent listener. People are not ready to hear you until you can be trusted to hear them.
- Ask questions about the person's life—family members, occupation, etc.

3. Intrigue

Add intrigue. Jesus introduced a novel idea. "If you knew the gift of God and who it is that asks you for a drink, you would have asked him and he would have given you living water" (John 4:10).

- Arouse curiosity. For example: "Nine years ago I would have felt the same way, but since then my outlook on life has totally changed."
- Share your testimony.

4. Inquire

Make inquiries about the person. When the woman at the well expressed interest in obtaining this unusual water,

Jesus asked her to "go, call your husband and come back" (John 4:16). Jesus knew, of course, that the man she was living with was not her husband; it was this insightful inquiry that led her to wonder about how to worship God. In addition to conversation turners that pique interest, then, we must know how to direct the conversation into a presentation of the Gospel. Here are some questions to ask:

- "Do you have any type of religious background?"
- "Have your ideas about God changed since [coming to college, getting married, having children, being in this job, the death of your friend, etc.]?"
- "By the way, are you interested in spiritual things?"
- "What do you think a real Christian is?"
- "Have you come to a place in your spiritual life that, if you were to die today, you know where you would spend eternity?"
- "Suppose that you were to die tonight and stand before God, and He were to say to you, 'What have you done in your life to merit eternal life with Me and not eternal damnation?'"
- "What do you think is the greatest need that man has?"

5. Introduce

Introduce the person to Jesus. After the woman and Jesus had talked for a while, after He had shown interest in her well-being, after He had made personal observations about her life, after He had turned the conversation to the coming Messiah, Jesus revealed who He was: "I who speak to you am he" (John 4:26).

- Introduce the matchless Jesus, revealing who He is and what He has done. This is the core of the Gospel.

87

6. Invite

Invite the person to accept Jesus. The woman at the well was so overwhelmed by her encounter with Jesus that she left her water jar, returned to town and described her conversation to everyone she saw. Then she issued an invitation of her own: "Come, see a man who told me everything I ever did. Could this be the Christ?" (John 4:29). Scripture says that many of the Samaritans from that town believed in Jesus because of the woman's invitation to come meet the Messiah (see verses 39–42).

- Make sure that you give an invitation: "Do you want to receive Jesus into your life?" "Is there any reason why you cannot give your life to Jesus?"
- Lead the person in prayer.

7. Incorporate

Remember to help the person become incorporated into the Body of Christ. When Jesus' disciples returned, the Bible says they "were surprised to find him talking with a woman," but no one questioned Him (see John 4:27). Instead, after she hurried off to tell others her Good News, they encouraged Him to have something to eat. Jesus used that opportunity to teach His disciples about His true food—His mission—and how the fields are "ripe for harvest" (verse 35). Then He quoted the saying, "One sows and another reaps" (verse 37). Again, true reaping is not only leading people to Christ but helping them become incorporated into the life of a church.

- Give the person helpful ideas of churches to visit if you are familiar with the area, or give an invitation to come with you if appropriate. If you are in an unfamiliar city, you might recommend that the person find a church that preaches the Bible, that welcomes the Holy Spirit and that is really friendly. (You can also give the person the number of Global Harvest Ministry to receive names of good churches closest to him or her, 800-683-9630, or check the website at harvestim.org.)

Go Boldly!

Remember, the message we share is the Good News of eternal life. You are not speaking about a new car, soap powder, timeshare sale or your neighborhood home-owners association. Someone once said that the person with an experience is never at the mercy of a person with a theory. You have an experience with Jesus Christ that can never be taken from you. His life inside you is the only proof you need to be confident. You are giving this person the truth of the Gospel that can forever bring hope and life. That is powerful! Do so with great confidence and joy. Do not believe the lies or distractions of the enemy or cower to his assaults as you step forth. Rather, know that his time is short; he knows it. You are on divine assignment—and the gates of hell shall not prevail.

8

DIFFERENT STROKES FOR
DIFFERENT FOLKS

Evangelism is a process. Sharing the right message the right way at the right time in a person's life will make your efforts more successful. Since everyone is living at a different stage of readiness regarding the Gospel message, it is helpful to know the basic types of people you will encounter.

As I have expressed, I do not believe the evangelism process is complete with just a verbal confession of faith. God intends for us to be rooted and grounded in the faith, growing in the Lord, full of the Holy Spirit, plugged into a local church and so much more. This means that we, as people who have a desire in our hearts to evangelize, are instruments of God *to begin or further this process* in those we meet.

None of this is set in stone; these are merely guidelines to assist you. The most important factor when interacting with any person, of course, is to be sensitive to the Holy Spirit and how He is leading you. Here, then, is a brief overview of seven types of people you may encounter—some unbelievers and some believers—and insights for your approach.

The Careless Sinner

Charles Finney coined the phrase *the careless sinner* to describe someone who is indifferent to the Gospel. This person is usually completely uninterested in religion and the things of God, and may be agnostic. This one is called the careless sinner because she could not "care less" about God. Have you ever met a person like that? We all have. She may be a family member or someone close to you.

The best thing to do with a careless sinner is to lavish her with love. Although love and the character qualities that I have already emphasized are a "given" when you witness to anyone, with a careless sinner you have to be even more sensitive and loving. Since she could not "care less" about God, it is not doctrine or facts or hell that will win her over or "scare" her into believing something of which she has no interest or fear. This is the time to draw on the Scripture that says, "The goodness of God leads . . . to repentance"(Romans 2:4, NKJV).

There is something inside all of us that cannot resist love. Love alone may provoke "the care less person" to ask why you are so loving or what gives you the ability to love even when she does not respond. Charles Finney advocates sharing the Gospel with this kind of person when she is alone and in a good mood. He strongly suggests being sensitive to the Holy Spirit's lead and asking God's insight for that special open door to this person's heart. I would add that prayers directed at plowing the ground of the careless, hardened heart are especially vital.

The Concerned Sinner

The second type of person you may encounter is what Winkey Pratney terms *the concerned sinner*. The concerned sinner is concerned about or interested in spiritual things. He is curious about religion, but he thinks he is basically good and has no sense of conviction regarding his personal state before God. With the concerned sinner, the law or Scriptures can be used effectively.

I remember open-air preaching at California State, Los Angeles, while a young Armenian student listened intently. When I shared truths from God's Word, conviction came. Though he thought of himself as basically a kind person who had done nothing terrible in his life, he realized as he heard the Word of God that he needed Jesus. He saw that he did not fulfill the requirements of the law and that he was not right before God. He gave his life to the Lord that very day. Today, Henrik Nazarian is a faithful member of Harvest Rock Church and one of my very close friends. The Word of God deftly handled can bring the concerned sinner to conversion.

The Convicted Sinner

The third type is *the convicted sinner*. This individual knows that what she is doing is wrong, yet she continues to do it. One young coed who grew up in a Christian home was sleeping around with different men. She told me that each time she compromised her values, she came under deep conviction. Yet she did not stop her actions, and she would not change.

With a convicted sinner, the emphasis must be repentance. When I speak at youth rallies and crusades, many people are already convicted. I do not have to preach the law to them. They already know that they are not glorifying God. Instead, I tell them how much God loves them with an emphasis on the meaning of repentance and its importance. When I give an invitation a deep work takes place, and many repent and come to know Christ.

As I mentioned in the previous chapter, it is important to be clear that repentance is not feeling sorry for your actions. It is a complete turning away from anything that is sin. It is *changing your mind* about a thing.

It is more effective, for instance, to help young people understand that having sex before marriage damages the inner man and will keep them from wholeness and liberty, both now and when they are married. When they see that the purpose is not withholding pleasure but rather avoiding pain, then they can more easily change their minds and say no when they are tempted.

Simply telling someone not to do something usually has the opposite effect. It is like saying: "Don't think about chocolate. Don't think about chocolate." The more we try not to think about it, the more power we give it. Focusing on the temptation puts the responsibility on the flesh, and our success is small. Yet when we keep our focus on a decision of a renewed mind fueled by the power of walking in the Spirit, we can more readily put away "the sin that so easily entangles" (Hebrews 12:1).

When the Holy Spirit is moving powerfully and breathing upon revival as He is today in many places in the world, convicted sinners often run to the altars to get right with God. I once heard that the founders of The Salvation Army, William and Catherine Booth, would preach no-holds-barred repentance to the skid row drunks. The Booths made it clear that if the drunks listening did not give up the bottle, they could not come into the Kingdom. Many repented of drunkenness on the spot and became future officers of The Salvation Army.

The Confessing Sinner

The fourth type of person you may encounter is *the confessing sinner*. This person always confesses his sins but never changes because he does not know what it means to put his faith in Christ.

With the confessing sinner, we have to emphasize what Jesus has already done and explain that salvation is a gift that is to be received by faith. Faith needs to be defined as the "evidence of *things not seen*" (Hebrews 11:1, NKJV, emphasis added). The promise of forgiveness of sins, the promise of salvation and the promised gift of eternal life based on the *finished work* of Jesus Christ are the keys for reaching this individual. You need to help the person understand that salvation is a gift not based on his performance but on the sacrifice of a Savior. Salvation is available by grace and not through any merit of his own. He needs to understand that his own efforts will always fail. He must trust the Lord and give Him full control. Then you can lead the confessing sinner to surrender his life to Jesus as both Lord and Savior.

The Converted Believer

The fifth type of person is *the converted believer*. This person is converted to Christ, yet has done little else in her spiritual walk. Perhaps she attended a crusade or a meeting where she accepted Christ, but she either does not know the next step or has not taken it.

The message that I emphasize here is the importance of water baptism and the infilling of the Holy Spirit. Several years ago I asked Dr. Kriengsak, who was at that time the pastor of the largest church in Thailand (The Hope of Bangkok), what has been the key to his church's phenomenal success. He said immediately, "Water baptism." He explained that because Thailand is a Buddhist nation, the acid test of a person's conversion to Christ is his willingness to be water baptized. This public display of faith for many people means rejection by their families. Some, therefore, accept Christ and attend the meetings, but they are unwilling to step forward and be baptized for fear of such rejection. They are in reality serving two masters. If a person is willing to be baptized in water, you know the commitment is true and profound.

Pastors in India within our own Harvest International Ministry network of churches experience the same thing. (HIM is a network of more than two thousand churches and ministries around the globe committed to helping fulfill the Great Commission by "changing lives, transforming cities and discipling nations.") Minovah Nickelson, who oversees more than sixty churches in southern India, says that they do not count a person as a true convert until after water baptism. With more than 300 million Hindu gods and goddesses worshiped in India, many people are more than happy to add another "god" to the list—especially one as kind, loving and powerful as the Lord Jesus Christ. The defining moment for them is a baptism that says death to self and the old life, and accepts new life through one God alone—Christ Jesus.

It is also imperative to share with the converted believer the truth about the need for the Holy Spirit and how to receive Him. God intends for us to walk in victory and power as Christians and to demonstrate His Kingdom on earth. It is only through the strength of the Holy Spirit overflowing in us that we will have that ability and authority.

The Consecrated Believer

The sixth type of person is *the consecrated believer*. This person has been truly converted, baptized in water, delivered from demonic addictions and filled with the Holy Spirit. The message to this individual is to be actively committed and involved in a local church.

I am continually amazed how many people misunderstand this verse from 1 John and act on their misperceptions: Because "the anointing which you have received from Him abides in you, and you do not need that anyone teach you; but . . . the same anointing teaches you concerning all things" (1 John 2:27, NKJV).

You will find people everywhere who may be wonderful Christians, but they do not attend church. They keep to themselves, believing they receive all the teaching they need from their personal Bible reading and time with the Lord. They see no need for being part of the local church because of this verse. This is dangerous for a number of reasons, but primarily because there is no accountability to others if their understanding is in error. We know that interaction with others in the Body brings growth, even if it is difficult at times. Also, the Body misses out on the revelations and gifting that person has to offer, and the person misses the joy that only the family of God can bring. As a result, the whole Body suffers (see 1 Corinthians 12:21, 26). Encourage those you encounter who may not rightly understand.

The Commissioned Believer

The seventh type of person is *the commissioned believer*. This person is a disciple of Jesus, properly initiated into Christ and an active member of a local church. This person needs to be encouraged, trained, commissioned and released to fulfill the Great Commission.

Many churches fall into one of two categories that hinder the full release of a believer into the Great Commission. One category is the church that is so inwardly focused it misses the big picture of reaching out to others. It is content with the status quo, the present membership, and the comfort zone and fellowship just as it is. The church members reflect these values and are usually interested only in their own church's activities. People like this need to be encouraged to "think bigger." They need to see themselves as ministers in the workplace (see Ephesians 4:11–12; 1 Peter 2:9). They might want to take a class on world missions, go on a short-term mission trip or help out at an inner-city outreach. They might benefit from traveling to hear an evangelist speak or having their church offer an evangelism class. If you know a person in this situation, you could offer these suggestions.

The other type of church may be too outwardly focused. There is not enough personal care for the members to be rooted and grounded in love so that they are good representatives of Christ when they take the message to others. We must first love God and ourselves before we can truly love our neighbor with the Gospel. You might encourage a person in this situation to investigate good inner-healing classes. Again, the Kylstra's Healing House or the Sandford's Elijah House might be helpful. Some local ministries that work in deliverance and healing of root issues of the heart might also be available.

The Holy Spirit's Prerogative

Keep in mind that these are only principles and basic guidelines about types of people; the Holy Spirit can choose to do any work in any person at any time. The same is true of any carefully planned presentation of the Gospel message. The points may or may not go in any sort of order. While the Lord usually allows us to be a part of His equation in the salvation experience, He is always free to do a sovereign work of conviction and conversion.

During the Jesus People Movement—the revival born out of the late 1960s counterculture—it was easy to lead people to the Lord. It was miraculous. People might approach you to ask what time it was, and you might say, "It's time to get saved"—*and they would*! Similar sovereign experiences are happening today. People as varied as unsaved Muslims in Turkey and tribal peoples in remotest Africa are having dreams about Jesus. They then go to local Christians they know about, saying, "Tell me about this man I saw in my dream. I know He must be Jesus, but I've never heard about Him before and I want to know more." They are having amazing conversion experiences.

The easiest type of conversion is always the one where they ask you. This reminds me of an incredible prayer you can pray anytime: "Jesus, send me the ripe ones. Grant me divine appointments. Lead me to those who are asking, Lord."

Jesus has already told us that the fields "are ripe for harvest" (John 4:35). We are not to estimate that the harvest is "four months" away and take our time about it. The harvest is now, and the Spirit Himself is breathing on you with great favor as you go forth in greater wisdom, power and love.

9

PRAYING

FOR THE LOST

In the poetic words of Amy Wilson Carmichael,

> O for a passionate passion for souls, . . .
> That pours itself out for the lost!

There is power in praying for others unlike that of any other
selfless act. If Jesus Himself *always* lives to make intercession for us (see Hebrews 7:25), it must be both a powerful
tool and a great priority. For the King of kings to choose
this as His most vital and kind eternal labor of love, would
He not earnestly give ear to our prayers on behalf of those
around us?

In recent years, the concept of intercession has somehow
taken on a note of complication. Suggestions have surfaced
that you have to be called to this ministry or that only an
elite power team of specially trained "Spiritual SEALs"
qualifies. Because of this some have excused themselves

from heartfelt prayer that is natural for anyone filled with the Spirit of God.

While it is true that some people have greater anointing for entering deeper places of intercession, still, intercession is everyone's business. Intercession is simply praying for someone else. Petition is praying for our own needs; intercession is praying for the needs and interests of others. Biblical examples include many great leaders who offered prayers of intercession for their people: Abraham interceded on behalf of the inhabitants of Sodom (see Genesis 18); Moses interceded on behalf of the Israelites (see Exodus 32); Esther interceded on behalf of her people (see Esther 4).

As New Testament believers, we are a "royal priesthood" (1 Peter 2:9), meaning that we are all priests ministering to Jesus, our great High Priest. The primary function of priests is intercession for the people of God. When we focus those prayers on the lost, we enter what I call *prayer evangelism*. This is because it has just as tangible an effect in the spirit realm as witnessing to someone personally in the natural realm. It changes the spiritual equation.

We will talk in this chapter about praying for the whole world, but you do not have to start there. Even so, as you begin to stretch your spiritual muscles, God will enlarge your capacity. In turn, you will no doubt find yourself praying for more and more people as He enlarges your heart. Here are some ideas to help you fulfill this practical style of evangelism.

Pray for Your *Oikos*

J. Oswald Sander, the great missionary leader from New Zealand, once said, "It is doubtful that anyone is saved apart from the believing prayers of some saint." Think about it. You probably had someone praying for you before you came to know Christ. It may have been a friend or your parents. As someone once quipped, "If you have a praying grandmother, you don't stand a chance!"

Everyone has a circle of influence, and we can begin by praying for our unbelieving friends and relatives within that circle. That includes your immediate family, your relatives, your friends, your neighbors, your coworkers and those closest to you. In Greek, this is known as your *oikos*, or "household." It is your special realm for prayer, an important part of your mission field, which we will discuss in chapter 11.

There is no doubt that my parents were praying for me fervently—and that my dad in particular began crying out to God all the more desperately the farther I ran from Him. I remember once, during the height of my rebellious days, I barged into my parents' room without knocking and found them holding hands and praying. I knew that they were praying for me.

And they were not the only ones praying. One day, a godly Christian man saw my friends and me driving around the neighborhood, smoking marijuana. He came home and said to his family, "I saw Ché Ahn smoking marijuana with his friends. We're going to pray for his salvation before we eat." They continued to pray for me before eating their meals. Their daughter, Kelley, was my age and went to the same high school. When I accepted Christ and she heard about it, she came up to me with tears in her eyes and gave me a big hug. She told me how God had placed me on her family's heart, and how they had interceded for me every day. Now she was sharing in the fruit of their answered prayers and the joy of my salvation.

After Sue and I were married, we also began to pray for our *oikos*, and God brought us astonishing results. I can honestly say that since we began acting on this principle in the mid-1970s, all of our known relatives have come to know Jesus. I do not have words to thank God. I will tell you more about this experience in the principles that follow.

Have a Specific Prayer List

As the saying goes, "If you aim at nothing, you end up with nothing." Over the years I have learned to be specific. When Sue and I began to pray for our *oikos*, I targeted key family members to pray for by writing their names down on an empty page at the end of my Bible. I kept the list no longer than five names. I did that for a reason: I did not want to be overwhelmed by praying for all of my lost relatives every day. I wanted to have a specific goal that was "doable" on a daily basis. Then during my quiet times, along with reading the Bible, I moved into a time of prayer with specific focus on my list.

After a person on my list came to know the Lord, I replaced that person's name with another relative's name. I began with our relatives, basing that decision on the principle of putting your family first. I still pray through a specific list today. The names now are my non-Christian friends and the acquaintances God brings to me.

Add Power by Fasting

Sue and I added another powerful principle to our prayer evangelism for all of our unsaved relatives: We decided to fast and pray one day a week for them. We chose Tuesdays. We skipped breakfast and lunch and broke our fast with dinner.

Our discipline of adding fasting to our prayers was developed during our early years on the leadership team of a large Bible study in the '70s called T.A.G. or Take And Give—meaning take what we had and give it to others. As leaders, we were asked to pray and fast on the days of the meetings. We saw thousands come to know Christ during those years. We also learned about the power of prayer and fasting through the Jesus People Movement and its sweeping revival.

My personal commitment to prayer and fasting went to a new level when God directed Lou Engle and me to begin a ministry known as The Call in the year 2000. That was a clarion cry to the youths of America to come to the nation's capital to pray and fast for revival in our nation. They did not come for special music, great name attractions or most of the things that impress kids.

When we put out the invitation, we had no idea how many would respond, but God was moving on hearts all across our land. More than 400,000 people of all ages (though mainly youths) answered that call on September 2, 2000. They sat in sweltering heat twelve to fourteen hours a day with only water to sustain them, oblivious to anything except their desperation for God. That fasting and desperation broke the heavens. Out of that Call were many other Calls—they continue around the nation and the world—spawning not only more fervent, dedicated youths, but thousands of new believers lit by their passionate fires.

During The Call years, from 2000–2003, I probably fasted more than in all my other years combined. I am not trying to boast, because anyone who knows me knows that I hate to fast. I love food and it shows! (My wife tells me I am pleasantly plump.) I would joke with Lou during our early years of ministry, saying, "You do the fasting, and I will do the eating." Yet because of Lou's inspiration and the foundations laid by my early leaders, I learned the importance of fasting and have seen the incredible results. If I can fast, believe me, you can, too. God's grace *is* sufficient for anything. I believe the reason fasting is so important is that it takes us from the seen realm into the unseen realm. Our focus becomes what is born of the Spirit and not of the flesh. We deny ourselves, and God moves. We do not fast to force Him to move, but fasting is woven throughout the Word with a sobriety to see change.

It is interesting that God encourages us to pray with fasting, saying that when we do He will pour out His Spirit on all flesh (see Joel 2:15, 28). Then things really do change. We move into a whole new level of intercession when we add fasting to our prayers.

Experience the Power of Agreement

Jesus said in Matthew, "Again, I tell you that if two of you on earth agree about anything you ask for, it will be done for you by my Father in heaven. For where two or three come together in my name, there am I with them" (Matthew 18:19–20). I love what Kenneth Copeland teaches about this verse. He says, "You know why God answers the prayer of two people in agreement? I'll tell you why. He almost has to. How often do two people agree about anything?"

It is funny, but so true. We all have our own opinions, our own demands, our own agendas. Many times we just simply do not take the time to sit down with someone else and pray. Yet the truth is, incredible power is released when people agree together in prayer.

Once Sue and I started agreeing together in prayer and using the principles outlined here, it only took two years for us to see our entire list of known relatives come to Jesus, with one exception whom I will discuss in the next section. We still agree together in prayer every day. It is one of the most powerful things we do together in ministry. You can agree in prayer with your friends, your coworkers, your small group members or the participants in any prayer meeting as you break down into smaller groups. Or you can move into exponential agreement together as a local church.

One of the greatest testimonies of this type of prayer I have heard came from Pastor Jim Cymbala of the Brooklyn Tabernacle Church. I heard him tell this story at one of Jack Hayford's pastors' conferences some years ago.

Jim had a backslidden daughter who had a baby out of wedlock and was living with her boyfriend. She had left the church several years prior. Jim had a large congregation, but was going through a season of depression because his daughter was lost. One day, a church member came up to Jim and said that the whole church should agree in prayer for Jim's daughter at the weekly prayer meeting. Initially Jim was reluctant, not wanting to draw attention to himself and his problems. Eventually, he agreed.

That next meeting, the whole church agreed together and cried out in prayer on behalf of Jim's daughter. Early the next morning, Jim was shaving and getting ready as usual for the day. There came a knock on the door. Jim's wife opened the door and could not believe her eyes. Their daughter fell to her knees and grabbed her mother's legs, begging her forgiveness for all the rebellion and sins she had committed.

Then the daughter asked urgently, "Where is Dad?"

"He is upstairs, shaving," her stunned mom replied.

Quickly, she ran upstairs and knocked on the door. When Jim opened the door, he was shocked to see his daughter. She got down on her knees and began to weep and ask Jim's forgiveness for all the sins she had committed. Then she asked, "Dad, what happened last night?"

Jim had to think for a moment to reorient himself. Then he replied, "We prayed for you as a church. Why?"

She told him that in the night she had had a dreadful dream. "It was so real," she said. "I thought I had actually died—and I saw myself going to hell." The experience was so horrendous that she cried out to God and asked Him for a second chance. At that moment, she woke up and realized that it was a dream. She said that when morning came, the first thing she wanted to do was go to him and ask for forgiveness.

Jim's daughter radically repented and came back to Jesus. Her boyfriend also came to know Christ. Today they are married and both are working on the church staff. That is the power of agreement in prayer.

Persevere and Never Give Up

Some of you may have been praying for your family members for a long time and they still have not responded. Let me encourage you not to give up. Listen to what Luke 18:1 says: "Then Jesus told his disciples a parable to show them that they should always pray and not give up."

My uncle Mark's salvation is a classic illustration of the power of persevering prayer. My uncle was a successful businessman who came from a Buddhist background. Although he married my aunt, who came from a Christian background, and they attended my father's church, Uncle Mark had never responded to the Gospel.

Uncle Mark was also an alcoholic. When he drank, he became violent. For years, our whole family prayed for his salvation. I have to admit, when I put him on my "target list" in my Bible I thought he was the least likely person ever to convert to Christianity. God taught me a lesson, however, that no one is so lost that he cannot be saved. After twenty years of our interceding for him, he finally started to open up to the Gospel.

One day, my uncle and aunt had such a terrible fight they had to separate from each other. My aunt did not tell him her whereabouts. During this time, Uncle Mark saw a brochure that came in the mail for her. It was an invitation to a Benny Hinn campaign that was coming to Anchorage,

Alaska. My aunt had been dramatically changed by the ministry of Benny Hinn, so my uncle decided to attend the event in hopes that something would happen to him. He flew to Alaska, not knowing that my aunt was also in attendance at the event.

When Benny Hinn gave the altar call for salvation, my aunt saw my uncle walk down the aisle to give his heart to Jesus. Moreover, when he prayed the sinner's prayer, the Holy Spirit came upon him powerfully; he was the only one at the altar to fall to the floor under the power of the Holy Spirit. He has never been the same since. I hope this testimony encourages anyone who has been praying for a loved one or friend never to give up.

The classic illustration of persevering prayer for the lost is the testimony from George Muëller's life. George Muëller had five friends that he interceded for throughout his entire life. His first friend came to Christ after he prayed for him for five years. Two more friends were converted after ten years of intercession. Two more came to know the Lord after 25 years of prayer. Muëller prayed for his fifth friend for 52 years and died without seeing his conversion. But right after Muëller's death, his fifth friend gave his life to Jesus! No wonder Billy Graham believes that the secret to seeing souls saved in his crusades is prayer. I heard that he once gave the following three keys to his powerful crusades:

Number 1: Prayer.
Number 2: Prayer.
Number 3: Prayer.

There is no substitute for prayer when it comes to evangelism. Prayer births salvation—and all else in God's Kingdom. If it did not, Jesus would not spend His time devoted to it; nor would He call us to it.

Praying for Cities and Nations

Jesus called His Church a "house of prayer for all nations" (Mark 11:17). You can be standing at the sink in your kitchen doing dishes and change a nation through your Spirit-led prayers. You can gather with your friends and cry out for the faces of those you may never see to be saved half a world away. You can intercede for those locked behind the closed doors of oppression who may never hear the words of the Gospel, but who can receive a divine visitation or revelation from God Himself.

Prayer has no geographical boundaries when it comes to reaching the lost. Let me share with you how corporate prayer is bringing in the harvest in Nepal, an extremely difficult nation to reach for Christ. My good friend Lok Bandari is a member of the International Apostolic Team of Harvest International Ministry. I am privileged to serve as president of HIM and was speaking at the annual conference in Nepal to some of the 1,500 pastors and leaders Lok oversees. I was amazed at the growth in that nation because there was only *one* Christian in Nepal in 1950. Now there are more Christians in Nepal than in Japan!

Fascinated, I asked Lok to give me his insight on the booming harvest in his country. He took me into his office and showed me a graph of the national church growth of Nepal. There was virtually a flat line from the 1950s to the 1990s. In the 1990s, the graph showed an explosive growth spike upward that looked like Mount Everest. I asked him what happened in the '90s.

Lok replied, "Ché, two things happened. First of all, through the AD 2000 movement led by Louis Bush and Peter Wagner, people began to pray for the nations of our specific geographic area. Suddenly, we had millions of Christians—many of them Americans—praying for Nepal. Second, Korean missionaries came to Nepal and they taught us early morning prayer." Sure enough, during the pastors' conference nearly every leader in attendance came to 5:30 A.M. prayer.

Revival is breaking out all over the world where people make prayer a high priority. I have heard reports like this from India as well. Recently I was honored to minister to 120 key leaders of the House Church Movement in China. Every morning at five o'clock, all of the leaders were already in their places praying fervently. No wonder the church in China has grown from one million in 1948 when Communism took over to current estimates of 150 million strong. Africa is also exploding with revival and church growth. One movement in Nigeria gathers more than *one million* people for an all-night prayer meeting the first Friday of each month.

Such fervency is nothing new. Revival history has taught us that prayer is the key to every true revival. Historians have concluded that the Great Awakening and the Second Great Awakening were the direct results of continuous prayer. In 2004, we celebrated the centennial of the Welsh Revival, a revival fueled by the prayers of a young man named Evan Roberts. The Azusa Street revival of 1906, which is credited with spreading the Holy Spirit and tongues around the world, began as a prayer meeting in a small house in Los Angeles on Bonnie Brae Street.

Prayer is the underlying foundation of both our personal lives in Christ and the great moves of God. The Holy Spirit is moving to establish 24-hour houses of prayer around the world that I believe are helping to pray in the harvest as well as establish the Kingdom on earth. The Justice House of Prayer in Washington, D.C., led by my friend Lou Engle, is a great example of young people who are praying around the clock for our government and for our nation.

Using the same principles set forth in praying for individuals and believing for their salvation, you can help call forth eternal life in cities and nations around the world.

10

LOVING SERVICE

It was another hot, sultry morning in the nation's capital. A heat wave had claimed the lives of many elderly throughout the nation. It was already almost one hundred degrees at nine in the morning as I heard the trash truck drive up our road. Then I heard the Holy Spirit whisper into my heart to give the trash collectors something to drink. I went in search of Sue.

"Honey, do we have any lemonade?" I asked.

"No, but we have some orange juice."

I quickly explained my mission. Sue grabbed a stack of paper cups and gave me the pitcher of orange juice. I ran out of the house, placed the cups and the juice on the hood of my car, and chased after the collectors who had already passed our house.

They saw me waving them down. Trying to catch my breath, I blurted, "Guys, it's a hot day. I have some cold orange juice at my house. Why don't you take a little break? I'm just a few houses back."

They looked at each other incredulously. After all, who cares about trash collectors? After recovering from the shock of the invitation, they proceeded to follow me to the house.

I poured juice for the four sweaty but appreciative men. As they drank under the shade of our large oak tree, I began to converse with them. "You know, several years ago I would have never stopped to help anyone else. All I cared about was myself. You see, I was a drug addict. But a number of years ago, I surrendered my life to Jesus. He has completely changed my life. I just want to let you know that there is a God and He loves you very much."

The men smiled, thanked me for the drinks and then went back to work. No fireworks. No one got on his knees to repent. The Gospel was simply demonstrated through an act of service and a little testimony before the men resumed their duties. I forgot about the incident until a year later.

My wife and I had just bought our first home in a different area of the city and moved in. As we were unpacking our boxes, the trash began to pile into a considerable mound. Knowing that the trash workers had their job cut out for them, I had an idea on pickup day. Why not bless them with a little continental breakfast on our new patio? Sue and I took out some juice and different varieties of bread, arranged it all nicely on our patio table and waited for the trash collectors to arrive.

I met them in front of our house and said, "We just moved in. With all of the extra trash we have for you to take, we thought we could return the favor by inviting you men to a little breakfast on our patio."

You should have seen the looks on their faces. It was another "Is this guy for real?" look. They all complied happily and followed me to our patio. As they began to munch on their breakfast, I began to share my faith. "I would have never done this several years ago, but since then I have given my life to Jesus Christ and I—" Before I could finish the sentence, a beautiful African American interrupted me and said, "Didn't you used to live on Georgia Avenue?"

"Why, yes," I said, amazed. "But we just moved to this new house."

"You're the guy who gave me and my friends some orange juice on that hot summer day," he countered.

"Yes, I am," I answered, as that recollection became more clear.

"Well, I want to shake your hand," he said, reaching out his hand. "I want to thank you for sharing your testimony with me. You made such an impression on me that when a friend of mine invited me to a Christian conference a few weeks later, I went and gave my life to Jesus there. I want to thank you for planting that seed in my life."

I was stunned. I started to praise God for His goodness and faithfulness. At the same time, I began to smile at God's sense of humor. Who else but God could have orchestrated these events? Here was a man who came to know the Lord in part because he received a cup of orange juice. He was transferred to another neighborhood on his job. Sue and I bought our first home on his new route, and God allowed us to run into him and hear his testimony. I was blown away!

I also thanked God for that very incredible lesson on *servant evangelism*. Following the Holy Spirit's prompting to do such a small act of kindness on that summer morning had far more significance than I could ever have imagined. That is why it is vital to follow even the smallest nudge from God.

While miracle stories of salvation can sometimes sound more awe-inspiring, servanthood is one of the most consistent and solid foundations in winning the world for Christ. It was Jesus' way of saving the world. When the disciples

were arguing about who would be the greatest in the Kingdom, Jesus called His disciples together and said,

> "You know that the rulers of the Gentiles lord it over them,
> and their high officials exercise authority over them. Not so
> with you. Instead, whoever wants to become great among
> you must be your servant, and whoever wants to be first
> must be your slave—just as the Son of Man did not come
> to be served, but to serve, and to give his life as a ransom
> for many."
>
> Matthew 20:25–28

Jesus was teaching His uncompromising test of true
Christian leadership—namely that leaders are servants
first. This is something that every believer and Christian
church must embrace. It is time to quit leading like the
world and comparing ourselves with others. Fleshly efforts yield poor fruit. Everything Jesus did was contrary to
the way humanistic man chooses to do things. Man "lords
it over" those beneath him. Jesus served, and He gained
the trust and respect of those beneath Him. That is what
qualified Him to lead.

Jesus' method of reaching the lost was simple: He served
them, and laid down His life for them. The apostle Paul, one
of the greatest evangelists and church planters in history,
had the same approach: "I make myself a slave to everyone,
to win as many as possible" (1 Corinthians 9:19). Servant
evangelism can revolutionize the world.

A good example of servant evangelism is found in a
Vineyard church in Cincinnati founded by Steve Sjogren.
They do practical things for free to bless others: They clean
bathrooms of local businesses; they wash people's cars; they
put money in expiring parking meters and leave notes saying they just wanted to show God's love in a practical way
and ask if there is any other service they can render. Can you
imagine the shock on people's faces to be so blessed?

113

People never forget acts of loving service. Think about your favorite teacher in elementary school. Can you remember what she taught? What made her special was most likely due to the kindness and acceptance she *demonstrated*. That is why Spirit-led servant evangelism can be a powerful way of reaching the lost. This is not to minimize preaching. People just need to know you care about them. You do not need to keep preaching the Gospel or giving the Four Spiritual Laws over and over again when people see your servant character. Besides, most people probably remember that you told them those things. They have been watching ever since.

St. Francis of Assisi once said, "Preach the Gospel at all times, and if necessary, use words." In this day and age, it truly is extraordinary for someone simply to do something kind for someone else without a motive. Allowing someone that is in an obvious rush to go in front of you in line at the grocery store or ticket counter is servanthood. Looking for ways to help your neighbor or lend things that others need is servanthood. It is a great witness to bring dinner to a sick neighbor or mow the grass of someone who is out of town or care for the pets of those on vacation. Each act of service is an opportunity to show Christ's love. When people see that, they often say, "Now, tell me about your Jesus."

Consistent servanthood is impossible apart from the grace of God and Spirit-led living. Servanthood does not come naturally for me, and perhaps many others, but it can be learned. It does require sacrifice and practice.

I remember once I was preparing a Sunday sermon on servanthood. Sue came into my study and asked if I could go to the store for her. I responded by saying, "I can't right now because I'm preparing this important message on servanthood." Ridiculous, I realize, but true. My wife is just the opposite. I often joke by saying if you want a definition of servanthood, look it up in the dictionary, and you will see Sue's picture.

Because of my weakness in this area, I have asked God to help me to become more of a servant. He has taught me three things you might find helpful:

1. Embrace the value of being a servant. Contrary to the world's view, we need to understand the high honor of servanthood. We must esteem the biblical conviction that the privilege of being conformed to Christ's image specifically involves the honor of being like Him in serving. If you are called to any level of leadership, you especially need to embrace the call of being a servant first.

2. Strive to obey the Holy Spirit's leading. I will say this again and again: The key to successful evangelism (or anything else, for that matter) is to find out what God is doing and then join Him. There have been a number of times, for example, that the Lord has led me to pick up the restaurant tab of a total stranger—and then leave a tract or share with that person a brief reason why I am doing it. God knows the states of people's hearts, the timing involved and what seeds need to be planted. Our job is simply to be open, loving and obedient. One really great example of "power servant-hood" is told by my friend and awesome prophet-ess Cindy Jacobs in her book *The Supernatural Life*. Cindy had just returned from church when she was summoned by her neighbor's child to come and pray for their very sick horse. She was overdressed for climbing under the barbed-wire fence and tromping through the field to the barn, and, frankly, she did not want to make the trip. But she felt the Lord tugging at her heart with the idea that praying for the horse just might open her neighbor's heart to receiving the Lord. She had looked for occasions to win the little girl's dad without prior success. This was the door. As she prayed, the horse immediately and miraculously

stood to his feet. That act of kindness (and power) did indeed soften the man's heart—which led to his salvation. He now serves as a leader in his church.

3. Serve with the talents and gifts He has given you. I believe every Christian has been given spiritual gifts. We should use our gifts to serve the lost. If you have the gift of hospitality, for instance, reach out by inviting people into your home. I know many people who love to invite international students to their homes for dinner, especially for American holidays. This gives a great opportunity to show love and introduce Christianity in a more relaxed setting.

Your gift is just as vital if it is not what some term a "spiritual gift." Teens need help with their homework. Folks need help with their taxes. Your talent may be fixing cars or roofs or plumbing. When someone needs help with these things, it is every bit as much Christ's love being shared as if it were a prophetic word or a healing.

Whatever your gifts of service, share. Open the door to salvation. "Love never fails" (1 Corinthians 13:8).

11

YOUR TARGET
MISSION FIELD

I love evangelism. I love all sorts of evangelistic methods. I love puppet evangelism, power evangelism, street evangelism, phone evangelism, sports evangelism, crusade evangelism . . . you name it, I love it! But I do believe that there are certain methods that work more effectively than others. Those are the methods I love most because I love seeing God glorified with the greatest number and the most lasting of commitments.

While I believe that God is leading His people to evangelize in great moves where His Spirit is breathing, we also often have the opportunity of choosing our mission field. The best place to start is right in your own backyard.

Friendship Evangelism

When approaching evangelism on an individual basis, the bond of friendship makes the best and most lasting converts—

on average 80 percent maintain their commitments! When you share the Gospel with friends, they are more likely to feel that a "genuine" Christ has been presented to them for the right reasons. When you reach people you know, they are more likely to become members of local churches and stay committed to the Lord because of the relationships developed there. It generally takes about five exposures to the Gospel message before a person accepts Christ; this is most easily done in the context of a friendship.

Those who have studied "failed conversions" reveal, conversely, that people who accept Christ at nonrelational events, such as traditional crusades or large meetings where they have no friends involved, are highly likely not to pursue the Lord. (Some statistics show that only 1 percent of the harvest is retained.) Seventy percent of those led to Christ by a stranger will drop out of the church. A full 90 percent of those people report feeling that the Gospel presentation they received was manipulative. If they do attend church but no meaningful friendships are developed, they generally leave. (For further information see *Gentle Persuasion* by Joseph Aldrich.)

The reality is obvious! *Friendship evangelism* is one of the most effective ways of reaching the lost.

I have seen this in my own life through the years. I have often had the privilege of leading people to the Lord who have been lovingly prepared by the patient friendship of other Christians. I remember one man named Mike who had a Christian wife and some outstanding Christian friends. A number of years of patient sowing on their part went into his life. I remember talking to him early in our relationship when he was simply not ready. His friends and wife continued lovingly to sow into his life. He was a plumbing contractor, and one day he came over to fix our sink. As we talked I could see that the Holy Spirit was drawing him. I shared the Gospel again and asked him if he would like to pray. That was the day! Right there in my kitchen he repented and gave his heart to Jesus. He is now a leader in his local church and one of the most outstanding Christians I know.

In another instance years ago, my sister, Chung-Hae, and I reached out to her friend named Tom. Tom was in one of my college history classes. Both my sister and I loved him and shared the Gospel with him. After graduation, I lost track of him. I was surprised one day to receive a letter from him. Here is a quote from the letter:

> Dear Ché,
>
> I'm not sure if you remember me, but many years ago I used to commute to work with your sister, Chung. These also were my college years at the University of Maryland, and I had the providential opportunity to witness the spiritual experiences of you and Chung. Seeing Christ in both your lives left a mark on me that has never left.
>
> In 1985, I decided to totally and completely devote my life to Jesus Christ. I could enumerate the many blessings Christ has since given me; and maybe the Lord will allow our paths to cross and we can do just that. However, my purpose in writing you and Chung is simply to thank you for your concern for me so many years ago and to be encouraged, your work was not in vain!
>
> In Christ,
> Tom

More recently, I was speaking at a conference that Peter and Doris Wagner were hosting in Denver. (Dr. Wagner, formerly a professor at Fuller Seminary, is founder and president of the Wagner Leadership Institute in Colorado Springs.) After I spoke, a woman came up to me and told me that she had been a friend of Chung-Hae at Smith College. She said that she had attended an evangelistic meeting that my sister had organized at the school. She wanted me to know that I had preached that night and that she had given her life to Christ. My sister had lost track of her, but some thirty years later she was still walking with the Lord. If my sister had not befriended this person, she would probably never have shown up at the meeting where she ended up meeting her Savior.

This style of ministry blends well with what we learned earlier about lifestyle evangelism. It is simply you being you and doing what you do every day. It is not about being a "superstar" but about being personable and personal. It is about sharing the Christ in you and loving someone to the harvest—whether it means planting the seed, watering what someone else has sown or being the harvester. It means being around for the long run.

Why We Hesitate

If friendship evangelism is so effective, why aren't more Christians befriending sinners? We know Jesus did (see Luke 15:1–2). I believe that the main reason is time. We all lead busy lives, yet as I mentioned earlier, reaching the lost is *the one thing we have only this lifetime to do*—and the results are eternal.

I suggest adding evangelism to the list of things you may already be doing—talking with your neighbors; making friends at the gym; taking part in political action groups, business and professional associations, athletic teams, school volunteer groups and more. If you are not involved in any of these activities, join something!

And do not be concerned that involvement with groups like these is too worldly. We have already taken a look at Jesus' friends. The key is the difference between isolation and separation. We are to be *separate* in the sense that we are not to participate in sinful *acts* of the world, but we are not to be *isolated* from the people. We are ambassadors for the King of kings, so join in.

Another reason is effort. It does take sacrifice. As someone once said, "Witnessing is never convenient." I know many times when I feel the nudge of the Holy Spirit, I have my mind on other things. I would really rather go and get them done than stop and share about the Lord. I have to make a conscious effort to realize the nature of my choice, and choose to do it. Every single time I make that choice, I am never disappointed. Neither is the Lord.

It might mean answering the phone when you do not feel like talking. You might have to turn off the television or put down your favorite book. You might find yourself interacting with someone at the mall or office when you are in a rush to get home. It might take time on your day off to help an ill neighbor with yard work. It might mean overcoming that awkward moment of sharing the Gospel with your buddy when you would rather be talking about sports. Just do it. You will be glad you did.

A final reason we may not pursue friendship evangelism is the fact that many of us want guaranteed results. We do not want to make an investment unless we know that the person will indeed come to Christ. Jesus never gave us such a guarantee. He never had one when He died on the cross. All that He is asking is that in obedience and love, we share the greatest news ever known.

Where to begin? Begin with those closest to you. As we saw in our study of *oikos*, there is great fruit in befriending your family members. The Bible cites numerous examples of families and entire households coming to Christ: Cornelius and his household (see Acts 10:1–2, 44); Lydia and her household (see Acts 16:14–15); the Philippian jailer and his household (see Acts 16:31–34); Crispus and his household (see Acts 18:8); and Stephanus and his household (see 1 Corinthians 1:16). I am so grateful that my whole family is walking with Jesus and serving Him in some capacity.

Next reach out to those around you: neighbors, work associates, fellow students. Most everyone appreciates a cup of coffee, home-baked bread or an invitation to dinner as an icebreaker. Be yourself and love them. Share Christ naturally as the relationship evolves. That is what they need most.

From Your Backyard to the World

To those with more ambitious hearts, as John Wesley once said, "All the world is my parish." My purpose in writing this book is to address spiritual hunger and the mandate of evangelism on many different levels. It is time now to take a look at the broader picture—that for which I am giving my life: taking the Gospel to *all* the world. Here are two keys to best target this mission field.

Go Where the Spirit Is Already Moving

The harvest is now. Jesus urged us to open our eyes and look at the fields (see John 4:35). That means we need to find out where the Holy Spirit is moving and go reap. One easy way is to look at where churches are growing. This applies locally and broadly, and usually indicates a move of God in the area.

When revival broke out in Argentina in the late 1980s and 1990s, the harvest truly overtook the reapers. When I visited there in 1991, I saw one congregation that had 140,000 members. The people held services 23 hours a day, seven days a week, to accommodate the crowd. They were begging the American pastors to send hundreds of church planters immediately to come and help their nation handle the harvest. It only makes sense to evangelize where God is already moving.

Revivalist Randy Clark, credited with bringing the move of God to Toronto, believes that God is now targeting Brazil and India as the fields most ripe for harvest. I believe God is stirring a multitude of nations and it will only increase as the momentum spreads. I recently heard Peter Wagner say that the five "hottest" spots in the world today are China, India, Indonesia, Nigeria and Brazil.

Find Out What Is on the Lord's Heart
and Reap There

We are watching as tremendous harvests are gathered in Mozambique through Iris Ministries. My good friends Rolland and Heidi Baker started in 1995 with a rundown orphanage and the goal of planting a church. After their powerful experience with the Holy Spirit in Toronto, which I will describe further in chapter 14, they became much more sensitive to the Holy Spirit's ways and seeking what was on the Father's heart.

In prayer they sought God's direction for what He wanted to do in Mozambique. He showed Heidi that His heart was for the children—AIDS orphans who had literally been thrown away because there was no one to care for them. She began visiting some of these children at the huge dump where they lived. Having no place else to go, they knew that at least there they could hope to find a dirty scrap of food to keep them alive. Her first church was planted with these children in a dump.

The Bakers then established a school to educate the orphans. That school has been rated by the government of Mozambique as the finest in the nation. These former "throwaway" children—mostly abandoned AIDS orphans—are graduating from college and getting good jobs. They are bringing amazing transformation to the government and business world. (*Always Enough* by the Bakers tells their amazing story.)

One of God's most extraordinary concerns right now is reaching the orphan, the widow and the poor. Those who share the Gospel with these whom He loves are reaching into the Father's heart, and I know the harvest will be great.

Another area that breaks God's heart is seeing His young sons and daughters in distress. Fear and hopelessness grip this emerging generation. A sense of purposelessness eclipses their sense of destiny. Untold millions are fatherless—if not literally, then emotionally. What God has called to be a covenant Elijah generation is being stolen or silently destroyed right in front of our faces. Yet many people would rather go and evangelize a Brazilian factory worker than share Christ with the kid down the street.

It is a known fact that most people accept Christ before they are 25 years old. In fact, two-thirds of all decisions happen before age eighteen. If you are not sure about a harvest field, let me tell you: This is indeed the Father's heart and will. Most young people do not have a clue about a God who loves them and a Savior who can make a difference in their lives. Perhaps that is why suicide is a top cause of death among teens.

I believe this emerging generation is called to be the carrier of the greatest revival in the history of mankind—if we will reach them with the truth. Sue and I are totally committed to reaching our youths. Let's do it together. "Even when I am old and gray, do not forsake me, O God, till I declare your power to the next generation, your might to all who are to come" (Psalm 71:18).

Be Willing to Sow in Hard Ground

In many places, it may take years to plow the hard ground so that salvation can come. This is most true in Muslim nations and those nations less reached with the Gospel. Many of these countries lie in what has come to be known as the "10/40 window." This window is a geographical area of latitude running from North Africa on the west to Japan and the Philippines on the east. It contains countless millions of people who have rarely, if ever, heard the Good News. Moreover, as I said earlier, there are still a thousand people groups throughout the world who have never heard the Gospel. If that is where God is leading you, that is where you will be most satisfied and fruitful.

POWER
EVANGELISM

12

THE HOLY SPIRIT'S MISSION

The late John Wimber, founder of the Association of Vineyard Churches, coined a wonderful term some twenty years ago: *power evangelism*. He wrote a groundbreaking book by that name. He was a pioneer in helping the last generation understand how the giftings we have in the Holy Spirit are the most powerful tools we can employ in sharing the Gospel. His message, however, was not new—just perhaps forgotten.

We know that Jesus Himself received the Holy Spirit, coming upon Him as a dove at His baptism in the Jordan (see Luke 3:21–22). The Spirit led Jesus into the wilderness to be tempted, and He overcame all temptation. Jesus then returned from the wilderness in the great power of the Spirit (see Luke 4:14) and began His ministry in the miraculous.

Even though Jesus' disciples were with Him throughout His entire earthly ministry, they, too, needed something more. As I mentioned earlier, He commanded them to receive the power of the Holy Spirit by waiting in the upper room (see Acts 1:4, 8). With this gift, the "apostles performed many miraculous signs and wonders among the people. . . . [And] more and more men and women believed in the Lord and were added to their number" (Acts 5:12, 14). The apostle Paul declared, "My message and my preaching were not with wise and persuasive words, but with a demonstration of the Spirit's power" (1 Corinthians 2:4).

The Holy Spirit has always been God's intended means of bringing a visible demonstration of His Kingdom to this earth. The Gospel was never meant to be dependent upon the words of man alone—no matter how eloquent or well intentioned.

Yet many people still believe that such powerful work of the Holy Spirit as I have just described has ceased. Most notably, cessationists believe that the miracle-working power and distinct infilling of the Holy Spirit were necessary to establish the fledgling Church. Now that the Church is established and the canon of Scripture is closed, cessationists believe that such power manifestations or infillings as I describe in this book are no longer necessary or available. They have ceased.

Perhaps you are among them. Or perhaps you believe that the Holy Spirit is at work in the world, but you have not yet considered asking for this gift yourself. You may already move mightily in the Holy Spirit and simply desire further empowering. In this section we will explore the mission of the Holy Spirit. We will discover truths about filling and refilling, and we will witness the signs and wonders He is performing all over the world, which I believe are available to all who will seek after them.

Let's begin with some inspiring experiences of well-known modern era Christians who received a distinct filling of the Holy Spirit. Their evangelistic influence for Christ increased exponentially afterward. This experience is captured by many different terms and phrases, including *being baptized with the Holy Spirit, receiving the gift of the Holy Spirit, being filled with the Holy Spirit.* Regardless of the terminology, the bottom line is that each of these believers received the *power* of the Holy Spirit.

I emphasize the word *distinct* because the experience of receiving the Holy Spirit most often happens at a completely different time following someone's conversion experience. I personally believe God's optimum plan is for this to happen at the *same time* one is saved (see Acts 2:38), but the overwhelming majority of the testimonies I have read or heard, including these stories that follow, seem to indicate otherwise.

Take D. L. Moody. I have read many accounts of how this famous nineteenth-century evangelist received the power of the Holy Spirit, but this description by the late author Catherine Marshall (*The Helper*, Chosen, 1978) is my favorite.

The year 1871 saw Dwight L. Moody apparently a great success as an evangelist. His tabernacle drew the largest congregations in Chicago. But according to Moody's own estimate of those years, he was "a great hustler" and this work was being done "largely in the energy of the flesh."

Two humble Free Methodist women, Auntie Cook and Mrs. Snow, used to attend these meetings and sit on the front row. Moody could not help seeing that they were praying during most of his services. Finally he spoke to the women about it. "Yes," they admitted, "we have been praying for you." "Why me? Why not for the unsaved?" the evangelist retorted, a bit nettled. "Because you need the power of the Spirit," was their answer. After this, Mr. Moody invited the women to his office to talk about it. "You spoke of power for service," he prodded them. "I thought I had it. I wish you would tell me what you mean."

So Mrs. Snow and Auntie Cook told Moody what they knew about the baptism of the Holy Spirit. Then the three

Christians prayed together—and the women left. From that hour "there came a great hunger in my soul," Moody was to say later. "I really felt that I did not want to live if I could not have this power for service."

One late autumn day in 1871 Dwight L. Moody was in New York (on his way to England) walking up Wall Street. Suddenly, in the midst of the bustling crowds, his prayer was answered: The power of God fell on him so overwhelmingly that he knew he must get off the street. Spotting a house he recognized, Moody knocked on the door and asked if he might have a room by himself for a few hours. Alone there, such joy came upon him that "at last he had to ask God to withhold His hand, lest he die on the spot from very joy."

From that hour Moody's ministry was never the same. He went on to England for what was to be the first of many evangelistic campaigns there. People thronged to North London to hear him. "The sermons were not different," Moody summarized. "I did not present any new truths, and yet hundreds were converted. I would not now be placed back where I was before that blessed experience if you should give me all the world." The evangelist was to live another twenty-eight years, and "to reduce the population of hell by a million souls."

Charles Finney, one of the greatest evangelists of all time, shares in his autobiography, *Memoirs of Rev. Charles G. Finney* (Revell, 1876), how the Holy Spirit came upon him after he returned from revisiting the woods where he was converted:

I returned to the front office, and found that the fire that I had made of large wood was nearly burned out. But as I turned and was about to take a seat by the fire, I received a mighty baptism of the Holy Ghost. Without any expectation of it, without ever having the thought in my mind that there was any such thing for me, without any recollection that I had ever heard the thing mentioned by any person in the world, the Holy Spirit descended upon me in a manner that seemed to go through me, body and soul. I could feel the impression, like a wave of electricity, going through and through me. Indeed it seemed to come in waves and waves of liquid love; for I could not express it in any other way. It seemed like the very breath of God. I can recollect distinctly that it seemed to fan me, like immense wings. No words can express the wonderful love that was shed abroad in my heart. I wept aloud with joy and love; and I do not know but I should say, I literally bellowed out the unutterable gushings of my heart. These waves came over me, and over me, and over me, one after the other, until I recollect I cried out, "I shall die if these waves continue to pass over me." I said, "Lord, I cannot bear any more"; yet I had no fear of death.

Aimee Semple McPherson was a remarkable healing evangelist in the early twentieth century and the founder of the Four Square denomination. This account was written by Daniel Mark Epstein in *Sister Aimee* (Harcourt Brace Jovanovich, 1993):

Aimee . . . took up her vigil kneeling by the Morris chair. . . . It was there she heard God's voice: "Now child, cease your striving and begging; just begin to praise Me, and in simple childlike faith, receive ye the Holy Ghost." Aimee did what she was told. She whispered, "Glory, glory," and each time the word seemed to come from a graver source within her and in a deeper voice. At last the words of praise came thundering out of her, resonating from her feet to her diaphragm and out the top of her head. Her hands and arms began to twitch and tremble, gently at first and then more violently, and then her whole body was shaking with the power of the Holy Spirit. She recalls that this seemed altogether natural; she had seen how the storage batteries she experimented with in school hummed and shook and trembled under the power of electricity. Her image is precise, and weirdly modern. . . . She trembled, and she quaked, until at last she slipped to the floor and "was lying under the power of God, but felt as though caught up and floating upon the billowing clouds of glory.". . . Then her tongue began to move in her mouth . . . vowels came howling and then a distinct syllable, and another, stammering, until they flowed in a sentence Aimee could not understand. "Then suddenly, out of my innermost being flowed rivers of praise in other tongues as the Spirit gave utterance" (Acts 2:4).

My final favorite is that of Billy Graham (my hero!). William Martin's outstanding biography of Dr. Graham, *A Prophet with Honor* (Morrow, 1991), gives this account of his being filled with the Holy Spirit:

> Billy was visiting Welsh evangelist Stephen Olford and Olford shared with Billy his experience with the Holy Spirit . . . those marvelous eyes glistening with tears, and he (Billy) said, "Stephen, I see it. That's what I want. That is what I need in my life." Olford suggested they "pray this through," and both men fell on their knees. "I can hear Billy pouring out his heart in a prayer of total dedication to the Lord. Finally, he said, 'My heart is so flooded with the Holy Spirit,' and we went from praying to praising. We were laughing and praising God, and he was walking back and forth across the room, crying out, 'I have it. I'm filled. This is the turning point in my life.' And he was a new man."

The year was 1947, a year before Billy would be catapulted into international fame as the greatest evangelist of modern time.

These are just a few examples of the infilling of the Holy Spirit—the same power shaking lives today that shook the world at Pentecost. It is a gift *for* us, to reside *within* us and to bless us. Yet most importantly, the Holy Spirit is to work *through* us for the benefit of others—a benefit unparalleled in exponentially fulfilling the Great Commission through love and power. Nothing could be more vital. Let me show you what I mean.

13

SOAKING WET

The invitation to join my friend's youth group on a trip to Buffalo, New York, came at a good time. Billy was one of the few Christians I knew after my dramatic conversion in 1973. Now it was nearing Easter of 1974 and I was lonely and longing for fellowship.

The trip was sponsored by a conservative evangelical Presbyterian church in nearby Silver Spring, Maryland. The high school and college students would leave on the Friday before Palm Sunday, do some sightseeing, and then on Sunday visit two Presbyterian churches in the Buffalo area before returning home on Monday. I did not know any of the students in the youth group except for Billy. This seemed like a great opportunity to meet other Christians and find out if I wanted to be involved with their church. And a promised sightseeing trip to Niagara Falls was very appealing. So I accepted. I had a simple, logical agenda.

God had other plans.

The trip up was good, and Niagara Falls was truly amazing. Yet I found myself hungry for God and looking forward to the Palm Sunday services. The first one was held in a large, dynamic church. I remember little about the church itself. I do recall that the senior pastor was an enthusiastic evangelist who had a television ministry. The Sunday morning service aired live and was inspiring in its joyfulness.

That evening, we joined the other congregation. This experience was quite disappointing. I do not recall any life in the church or any sense of reverence for the Lord. I say this not to be critical, but to show the difference when the Lord's presence is not really welcomed. During the offering, for example, two teenagers got up to sing a hymn together. They sounded horrible and they knew it. I think this may have been a "forced" youth event since our youth group was visiting. After hitting one wrong note after another, they started laughing at their mistakes right in the middle of their hymn presentation. With an air of flippancy, they abruptly stopped singing and sat down still laughing.

After the service, we all went downstairs to the fellowship hall to have some refreshments. I remember asking some of those young people if they knew Jesus. They did not know Him, they were not interested in knowing Him and they made it clear! I felt powerless in my witnessing endeavors and sad for these young "church" teens who did not know and did not care about the God who loved them.

Later our youth group gave a singing presentation for their congregation. We began with a popular song at the time called "Pass It On." Next we sang "Day By Day" from the musical *Godspell*. This song (later revived by DC Talk) is one of those songs I believe God truly inspired to reach the lost. I remember singing the words that night as a prayer: "To see Thee more clearly . . . love Thee more dearly . . . follow Thee more nearly . . . day by day by day. . . ."

At that very moment, it was as if God and I were all alone in the room. I was aware of nothing else. Inside my heart was bursting, *Yes, God, that's my prayer! Lord, I really mean these words with all my heart. I'm not just singing them. God, I really want to see You more clearly. I really want to love You more dearly. And God, I really want to follow You more nearly, day by day.*

As I began to worship the Lord with these words, tears began to stream down my face. I sensed the deep love of God and the awesome presence of God. Then a remarkable tingling, electrifying sensation started to spread over my feet, up my legs, up to my head, through my arms and down to my fingers. The sensation was so intense I could not move my fingers. I tried to make a fist, but I could not. The numbing but glorious pulsing continued to increase until my tears of worship turned to sobs of joy. I knew that God was touching me, though I had never heard or seen anything like what was happening to me.

To say the least, I was making quite a scene. This was definitely not in my plans. I had come on the trip to make friends and see Niagara Falls. Now I felt as though I *was* Niagara Falls! The youth leader in charge came over and asked me politely to leave the room. I forced my body to move and found my way to the men's room where I continued to weep and worship. I sensed that God was anointing me for a purpose. I did not hear an audible voice or see anything, but I knew in my heart that God had heard my prayer of dedication and service. I knew that He was empowering me for serving Him. It became clear to me at that moment that He was calling me to full-time vocational ministry.

I will never forget how the Holy Spirit touched me that night. I call it a "further infilling" of the Holy Spirit and will explain why. This would certainly not be the last time I experienced a further infilling of the Holy Spirit in such a powerful way. (If you have not yet received this wonderful gift, please see Appendix 3: "Being Personally Filled.")

Further Infilling of the Holy Spirit

We must have the power of God in order to evangelize and to fulfill our callings. The early Church waited to be "baptized with the Holy Spirit" (Acts 1:5) and to receive "power when the Holy Spirit" came upon them so that they could be "witnesses [of Jesus] in Jerusalem, and in all Judea and Samaria, and to the ends of the earth" (verse 8). This was fulfilled at Pentecost (see Acts 2:4).

These believers received a further fresh infilling of power as recorded in Acts 4:31: "After they prayed, the place where they were meeting was shaken. And they were all filled with the Holy Spirit and spoke the word of God boldly."

In fact, the apostle Paul encourages us to be filled continually with the Holy Spirit: "Do not get drunk on wine, which leads to debauchery. Instead, be filled with the Spirit" (Ephesians 5:18). The word *filled* in the Greek is in the continual present tense, so the verse really reads: "Do not be drunk with wine. Instead be continually filled with the Spirit" or, as one translation reads, "keep on being filled."

Scripture often refers to us as "vessels" of the Lord (see Jeremiah 18, NKJV, for instance). The one thing about being living vessels is that we *leak*. We need refilling. We need refilling with water and food, joy and love, affirmation and communication. The same is especially true with the presence of the Lord in our lives through the Holy Spirit. The way we will "walk in the Spirit, and . . . not fulfill the lust of the flesh"(Galatians 5:16, NKJV) is to be continually *filled* with the Spirit.

This ongoing filling with the Holy Spirit is available to all believers. Countless people experience this blessing regularly. I ask God for a fresh filling every morning. I do not believe there is only one experience of baptism with the Spirit or one experience of being filled. I believe it happens many, many times in our lives. At critical junctures, the Lord will fill us with a greater measure, often with manifestations of a new filling, because we have come into a new season of revival or commissioning. These times are distinct and unforgettable fresh baptisms. One translation of "baptism" is *baptizo*, which means to overwhelm or make fully wet. This has certainly been the case for me.

Here are two examples of what I mean.

Receiving a Commission

I was living on the East Coast at the time. In fact, I was asleep. It was about four in the morning of September 2, 1982. As I was dreaming, I saw a six-foot-five African American who reminded me of Rosie Greer, the famous football Hall of Famer for the then Los Angeles Rams. He issued me a Macedonian type of call: "The Lord is calling you to Los Angeles and there will be a great harvest."

When I awoke with these startling words burning in my heart, I then heard a phrase from a song pass through my mind: "Revival is at hand." I began to feel wave after wave of the power of the Holy Spirit coursing through my body like electricity. I knew this was God transferring His power through me as He gave me a new commissioning in ministry and a fresh infilling of the Holy Spirit for what He was asking me to do.

I have not yet seen the great harvest in L.A. that I saw in the Jesus People Movement, but I know it will happen—and be even greater. In the meantime, our home church, primarily through Harvest International Ministry, acts as a sort of Antioch, sending the Gospel message to many nations.

Fill Me Again, Lord!

Another time the Holy Spirit "drenched" me was on my first ten-day water fast. On the ninth day of the fast I was having my regular quiet time when I received a mighty baptism of love. I was so overcome by the love of God and so filled with His goodness that I wanted to love and hug anything that moved. I knew I was not the source because I was giddy with His presence. I enjoyed every second of it and pray everyone can experience it.

I was, however, less than happy about how this encounter with a further infilling of the Holy Spirit started out for me. It was January 1994 at the Anaheim Vineyard. I was not in the greatest mood. I was fighting depression after going through possibly the worst year of my life. Lou Engle and I were attending a conference there when the Holy Spirit began breaking out in waves across the auditorium. You could see the presence hitting different sections: People—with no one touching or praying for them—would begin to laugh and shake spontaneously and uncontrollably. Lou was excited. I heard him say, "Ché, get ready. It's coming toward us." I wanted nothing to do with it. I was determined not to laugh.

God's presence was stronger than my determination. I not only laughed, I began rubbing the bald head of the man in front of me, who thought it was funny, too! I was inebriated in the Holy Spirit. Everyone was having a ball. The result? My depression lifted and I enjoyed Father God as never before.

Experiencing this kind of powerful and refreshing presence of God has become the norm rather than the exception for me since that time. Wherever the Holy Spirit is moving uniquely like this, I will go. That is why I have traveled to places like Argentina, Toronto, Pensacola, Africa, India, China and more. I believe these experiences are not meant solely to give us joy, but also to give us strength for the journey and have more than enough to give away to others. I know God wants to bless all of His children with the same love and power of the Holy Spirit (see Luke 11:13).

God never intended for us to fulfill the Great Commission in our own strength and power; the Holy Spirit's power is indispensable to evangelism. It was true of the early Church; it has been true of every generation since. It is especially true of us today. As the end of the age dawns and Christ's return nears, there is no way Christians can reach billions of lost souls without God's supernatural power. All of our best efforts throughout many centuries cannot do what the Holy Spirit can do in seconds.

In the next chapter we will learn specifics about being available for that power, and we will witness it in action through testimonies from around the world.

14

TAKING POWER
EVANGELISM
TO THE STREETS

What is the Holy Spirit saying and doing today? Where is
He moving in power? And what are the results?

Let's start with the broad sweep of the Spirit worldwide
in power evangelism—as seen in those individuals who are
in step with the new apostolic movement. (We will discuss
this movement in chapter 17, "New Apostolic Wineskins.")
This Spirit-breathed movement and its myriad of Spirit-
risen churches across the world have grown five times faster
than all other churches in the last thirty years. It seems to be
flowing naturally, its momentum building from the time of
its birth, which is credited to the Los Angeles Azusa Street
Revival of 1906.

The Harvest Worldwide

Looking at just a few testimonies from these types of churches and ministries, I find it easy to see why salvation is on the rise and new churches are increasingly needed to house the harvest.

Latin America

The Holy Spirit is moving in great power in Latin America, especially in Brazil, Columbia and Argentina. Since I am familiar with what is happening in Argentina, let me share what I have observed. For more than twenty years, Argentina has been ablaze with a fire that has spread to her continent and many other nations, including the United States. (George Otis Jr. has produced a fascinating video series called "Transformation," documenting these unprecedented revivals.)

I had the honor of visiting Argentina in 1991 for the first Harvest Evangelism Conference, which was hosted by apostolic evangelist Ed Silvoso. The second day of my visit, a banquet was given for the American delegation, and I had the privilege of sitting with Omar Cabrera whose church had eighty thousand members at that time. Omar has since died; that evening was a rare opportunity that I prize. My natural question was, "How did your church grow to that size?"

I will never forget his casual reply. He said: "Creative miracles."

Mind you, he did not say "healings" or even "miracles," but "creative miracles." A creative miracle is when God creates something from nothing or grows something back that was not there. Excited, I asked him for some examples. He said that there were so many, we would be there all night if he told me everything that God has done. But I persisted. "Please give me just one testimony so that I can take it back to America." Cabrera finally began to share.

"There was an unbelieving, desperate mother who brought her four-year-old son to our Sunday morning service. This boy was born without a urinary tract. He had a tube sticking out of his stomach with a bag, and he eliminated his urine that way." (This is known medically as a ureterostomy).

"After prayer, God created a brand-new urinary tract inside the boy's body," Cabrera said. "Now he can go to the bathroom normally. The whole village knew about this boy. When the word spread, people started to come to the house and ask for a 'demonstration' from the little child to see if a miracle truly did occur. The parents and the boy obliged, and now the whole village is a part of my church."

That, my friend, is power evangelism. One creative miracle by the Holy Spirit brings a whole village to know the Lord and become a part of the church.

South America's Billy Graham

Another man God is using to change the face of evangelism is a former Argentine businessman who was a full-time nuts-and-bolts manufacturer. (I love God's sense of humor.) It is estimated that in a mere ten-year period during Carlos Annacondia's initial outreaches in South America more than two million people made documented decisions for Christ. Many churches were begun as a result of his ministry in Argentina, with huge growth also occurring in the existing evangelical churches. Peter Wagner is credited with saying that Carlos "may be the most effective inter-denominational crusade evangelist of all time."

Knowing the powerless and divided state of the Church in his nation, Annacondia diligently sought God and the Word for keys to transformation through the Gospel. His hallmark verses became Mark 16:17–18: "In my name they will drive out demons . . . they will place their hands on sick people, and they will get well." Annacondia believes it is essential to meet the needs of those who come to the meetings, including demonic deliverance and physical healing as a part of the salvation message.

Several years ago our church had the privilege of hosting Carlos Annacondia for a crusade in downtown Los Angeles. Carlos is a compassionate man combined with a pure fire. For every crusade he leads, Carlos asks for two large tents—one for his prayer team to pray for every single person needing healing and the other for his team to pray for every person needing deliverance. In the actual meeting area he prays at the altar for those wanting to receive Christ, and many times he calls for those needing healing and deliverance to come forward as well. His authority is so great in the Spirit, however, that many are healed and delivered spontaneously while he is preaching. You can hear the cries of release from the audience all throughout the message.

Carlos knows that God's purpose in bringing His creation to Christ is to set it free. Carlos expects to see that at every meeting, and he sees it. He knows that God has given us authority over our enemy, and he takes it. (Note his confidence in the title of his incredible book *Listen to Me, Satan.*) He is a nuts-and-bolts businessman who takes God at His Word, and he is now powerfully taking souls for the Kingdom.

Africa

Another testimony to the Holy Spirit's transforming power in evangelism can be found with my friends Rolland and Heidi Baker, whom I told you about earlier. They had been overseas missionaries in various nations for about seventeen years and had planted four churches (of which, according to their own account, two were "weak"). They also had handfuls of converts. By many standards, this would be a great life accomplishment. By theirs, it was disappointing and almost fruitless.

An encounter with God changed it all. The Bakers went to the Toronto Airport Christian Fellowship (TACF), pastored by my good friends John and Carol Arnott, after hearing about the Toronto Blessing. Rolland went to Toronto to witness the renewal he was hearing so much about. He was so transformed that Heidi wanted to visit, and did so. To describe the Toronto renewal briefly, Father God pours out "liquid love" with a manifest physical (though invisible) presence of the Holy Spirit. This presence heals hearts and refreshes God's children in body, soul and spirit.

After years of minimal results and exhausting "self-effort" in ministry, the Bakers were astonished at what happened in their lives through God's impartation of love and power in Toronto. Heidi was so enveloped by the Holy Spirit's deep impartation that she literally could not move for seven days during her visit. Her husband or someone else had to carry her to the bathroom. She fasted from everything but water and stayed "glued" to the floor of the Toronto church.

The Bakers had begun ministry in Mozambique, where they moved in 1995 to reach the poorest of the poor. When they returned after their visit to Toronto, revival broke out. As of this writing, the Bakers, along with their team, have planted more than six thousand churches in Mozambique and throughout other parts of Africa. They reach Muslims primarily. In addition, they feed ten thousand people every day and care for more than three thousand orphans. And the numbers are growing.

Though Heidi Baker has a doctorate in systematic theology (another of God's humorous ironies), the evangelistic methods employed by their ministry are anything but conventional. You will never find their tactics in a seminary textbook on missions. They load a flatbed truck with a generator, a portable sound system, a movie projector and free food. They drive to a remote village, set up and begin to show the film *JESUS*, a two-hour docudrama about the life of Christ, to draw a crowd.

Most people in these remote areas have never seen a movie or even television. Thus, the whole village turns out to see the marvel. Then the team turns the projector off and begins to preach. Rather than a crafted sermon, Heidi or a team member will simply say, "Bring me your blind, the deaf and the lame. Bring us even those who have died. Our Jesus will heal the sick and raise the dead because He is God."

Without fail, God shows up. There is such an "open heaven" (or ready access to the Lord) in Africa and over the Bakers' ministry that when the sick come and are prayed for, miracles happen every time. I know this because I went to be a part of Heidi's team in an outreach in Bangula, Malawi, and saw it for myself. The first five deaf people I prayed for were healed instantly. I saw the blind given sight and the lame walk.

Now it was not by the prayers of professional ministers that these miracles were happening. These prayers were offered by "regular people" who had joined the team just for this ministry trip. They were American students or housewives or those who work in the marketplace. Yet their ministry was incredibly powerful. Why? Because it is the Holy Spirit's power that creates the miracle. This power has never been our own. It is available to all who are willing to believe it, receive it and give it away in faith.

China

Testimonies of astonishing examples of power evangelism also come out of China. Her church remains underground because of persecution, yet it has grown from one million believers to an estimated 150 million believers in just fifty years.

The first time I was privileged to go to mainland China and meet with the underground church leaders was in 1986. I traveled with Dennis Balcombe, who I believe will be recorded in Church history as a modern-day Hudson Taylor. In my opinion, he has had the greatest impact of any Westerner in China. I had the opportunity to meet in a hidden place with several key leaders of the underground church, and when I asked how it has grown so fast, their unanimous reply was, "Signs and wonders."

It continues today. I returned recently from a series of secret meetings in a rural area with hundreds of underground house church leaders in attendance. After one of my ministry sessions, one of the church leaders returned to his village and invited an unbelieving friend with stomach cancer to come to the next meeting. I knew nothing about it. The dying man told the church leader that he would follow Jesus if he was healed. He had not been able to eat in a long time. He was miserably bloated and in excruciating pain. He received prayer in the service along with several other people. After the meeting, he was able to go home and eat normally. The pain and bloating stopped.

The next day, he came back to the services and brought his wife and two adult sons. He told the house church leader that he and his entire family wanted to give their lives to Jesus right there. The demonstrated, visible power of Jesus through signs and wonders makes the Good News real. And salvation follows.

Holy Discontent

These stories show us the new evangelism; this is power evangelism. This is doing what we see the Father doing.

And the wonderful thing is that this is for everyone, everywhere. God wants to do many wonderful things through His people as we learn to move in power to evangelize. Great things are happening and we can all be part of it.

This being true, however, it is also true that these and other notable experiences in various parts of the world are the exception rather than the rule. Power evangelism and its attendant evangelistic results are, far too often, weak or nonexistent.

This seeming disparity is, I think, the reason that many believers are frustrated in the Body of Christ: They hear God's call to move in power and help bring in the harvest, but they see in their own situations a lack of evangelistic results. There is a "holy discontent," and I believe God is allowing it. It motivates us to reexamine what we are doing.

One problem we can identify up front is our approach to evangelism. So much of what is done in the name of Christian ministry is different from anything Jesus would have done. We plan or do what *we* think is good and then ask God to bless it. Jesus, as we have stressed, never operated that way. The source and the motivation for His actions were always Father God. Look at Jesus' words:

> Jesus said to them, "My Father is always at his work to this very day, and I, too, am working." . . . Jesus gave them this answer: "I tell you the truth, the Son can do nothing by himself; he can do only what he sees his Father doing, because whatever the Father does the Son also does. For the Father loves the Son and shows him all he does. Yes, to your amazement he will show him even greater things than these."
>
> John 5:17, 19–20

Human efforts are especially tiring and dangerous because what we begin in the flesh, we must maintain in the flesh. Then when we fall short, we become discouraged and burned out. If we continue, forcing our plans through anyway, we usually end up being narrow-minded and offensive and producing unhealthy fruit that does not last.

Guidelines for Moving in Power

The weekend in Buffalo, New York, changed my life forever. The Palm Sunday experience of receiving the Holy Spirit altered the whole equation of Ché Ahn. In the years that followed, I began to see people healed by the power of the Holy Spirit when I prayed for them. More importantly, people started coming to Christ. I had not led one person to the Lord prior to that experience with the Holy Spirit. After the baptism of power, people started getting saved everywhere I went. Granted, the seventies were a unique time; the Lord sovereignly poured out His Spirit all across the nation. But I was just thrilled that God could use me.

And He wants to use each of us in this "new thing" He is doing. He has been so faithful and kind to teach me in recent years how to move in power evangelism. Here are a few principles that I have learned along the way.

Be Led by the Holy Spirit

About a year after my "Niagara Falls" experience, I was driving home from spending a day ministering to troubled youths when I passed a large house with a wild party in progress. It was a warm summer weekend, and kids were hanging out everywhere. I sensed the Holy Spirit nudging me to park my car and go to the party.

I knew that I would not know anyone there, but I parked my car anyway. The kids appeared to be high school students, and I had just finished my first year at a nearby university. Age did not matter, though, because I knew that I was going to meet someone with whom I could share the Gospel. I was simply obeying the Holy Spirit's leading.

As I walked into the house, I could smell drugs. I recognized the sickening odors from my former drug days. Beer cans were strewn all over the hallway floor. I noticed people smoking marijuana and smoking angel dust through a water pipe, called a "bong," in the kitchen directly ahead.

I headed for the kitchen and walked up to a young man who was focused on his drugs. He had hair down to his shoulders; one ear was pierced and had a long cross dangling down.

"Hey, I like that earring," I said, trying to strike up a conversation. "But why a cross?"

He mumbled, "I think it's cool. Besides, I respect it."

I proceeded to share my respect for the cross by telling how Jesus had changed me, a former drug addict. I noticed that other people around him were listening, so I raised my voice and began to share my testimony with the ten or twelve people who were in the kitchen. I further began to tell how God was supernatural and how He had healed me of my allergies.

At this point, a number of people started to laugh. I am sure it was a combination of the drugs and the amusement of a Korean kid walking into a room full of strangers and talking about Jesus and His power to heal. At least I had their attention!

I noticed that one girl was not laughing. She spoke up. "Can God heal my back?"

"Why, what's wrong with it?" I asked.

"I've had three back surgeries, and I'm in constant pain. It hurts so much that I can hardly walk. I can't even bend forward."

"Well, let's pray and ask God to heal you," I said, suddenly getting nervous. (Under my breath, I was sending up a quick prayer to God, "O Jesus, You have to show up for this one! Help me!")

I walked up to the teenage girl, placed my hand on her back and began to pray. "Father, I pray that You would show those in this room that You are a supernatural God; that You're for real; that You sent Jesus Christ to die for our sins; and that You will save those who call upon You. Please heal this person. In Jesus' name, amen." (I call this "evangelistic praying" because you are sharing the Gospel in your prayer. It is a natural part of power evangelism because you are looking for the manifestation of a healing miracle to back up your witnessing.)

I looked the girl in the eye and asked, "How do you feel?"

She had a bewildered look on her face. She said quite soberly, though hesitantly, "I don't feel any pain."

"Really?" I said with surprise, exposing my own unbelief and amazement. "Your back doesn't hurt?"

"No. The pain is gone."

"Why don't you bend a little and see if you can touch your knees," I said.

She started to bend and, with ease, she touched her knees.

Someone yelled out sarcastically, "I don't believe this!"

The girl responded, "It's true, I could never do this before. The pain is gone!" Then she proceeded to touch her toes.

I felt I had done what the Holy Spirit had asked me to do, so I left. Yet I was somewhat disappointed that I had not led anyone to the Lord after such a powerful demonstration of His reality.

God, however, was not finished. As I walked out of the house, I took a deep breath of the fresh summer air. A girl came up to me and said, "I saw what happened inside, and I want to know how I can become a Christian." I could hardly believe what I was hearing. For the next half hour, we sat on the front lawn of the house. I shared the Gospel with her and led her to the Lord.

When I got into my car to drive home—or should I say float home—the whole evening seemed wonderfully surreal. Through this one event God taught me firsthand how signs and wonders can be used to His glory. He showed me how the power of the Holy Spirit is given to spread the Good News and bring people to Him. He showed me the importance of following His guidance, and the harvest that power evangelism brings. This was before I had ever read a book about this kind of thing or heard it preached.

Being led by the Holy Spirit and obeying Him is vital to moving in the power of God to evangelize. So if you feel that inner "tugging," park your car. Ring the doorbell. Make that phone call. Write that letter. Speak to that person. Go to that place. When you get there, do what He tells you. Lives may be changed—and so may eternal destinies.

Look for Open Doors

Someone once said that "you know a door is open because you don't bang your face on it as you walk through the doorway." When someone is not receptive to being prayed for or to receiving a word that I have been given by the Lord, I simply move on. I do not feel condemned or as though I have failed God in evangelism. I really believe it is called the "great co-mission" because we are co-laboring with God in this wonderful adventure.

I do, however, look for and follow the wisdom and example of leaders like the apostle Paul to find out what the Holy Spirit is doing and where He is doing it. The book of Acts gives us great examples of Paul sharing the Gospel only as the Holy Spirit opened and closed doors:

1. "When they came to the border of Mysia, they tried to enter Bithynia, but the Spirit of Jesus would not allow them to" (Acts 16:7).
2. "So they passed by Mysia and went down to Troas" (Acts 16:8).

3. "During the night Paul had a vision of a man of Macedonia standing and begging him, 'Come over to Macedonia and help us'" (Acts 16:9).
4. "After Paul had seen the vision, we got ready at once to leave for Macedonia, concluding that God had called us to preach the gospel to them" (Acts 16:10).
5. "One night the Lord spoke to Paul in a vision: 'Do not be afraid; keep on speaking, do not be silent. For I am with you, and no one is going to attack and harm you, because I have many people in this city.' So Paul stayed for a year and a half, teaching them the word of God" (Acts 18:9–11).

If the Spirit is not moving, I am not going to make things happen by myself. Having said that, I am constantly looking for an open door—whether it is in another nation or the local grocery store. Airports, restaurants, libraries, post offices and malls are all fair game. So are public officials, presidents, kings.

One of the quirky doors God seems to open for me quite frequently is evangelizing to celebrities (mostly at airports)—from singers to football players to some of the cast of *Star Trek*. What doors seem to be open for you? Special meetings with clients? Prayer needs in the setting of your business? Favor with neighbors or groups with which you meet? Fellow passengers on long bus waits or train rides? Take a more careful inventory of your everyday activities and you might be surprised at the opportunities you never noticed before.

I believe a person sitting on a bench looking depressed or crying is someone to talk with and to ask if you might pray. Someone looking rattled in a doctor's waiting room is another. A frightened child or people waiting for assistance on the roadside after a minor accident would certainly qualify. The neighbor next door who you hear has just lost his spouse, or the woman down the street who has just had a baby could both use some support. Those who have needs after a storm or power outage are a good choice.

Sometimes we overlook the people that are right around us who could use a demonstration of God's power. Jesus did not have to go far to find those who needed Him. In fact, after witnessing a few demonstrations of His love and power, they came looking for Him. Operate in these, and I guarantee people will come looking for *you*, and your fruit will multiply quickly.

Pray for Those Who Need a Miracle

One day, I was leaving my house to go to the church office. My neighbor Ann called out to me from across the street. Ann and her husband, Andy, were the typical California unchurched yuppie couple. Sue and I had reached out to them repeatedly, inviting them for dinner and keeping in touch, yet having little evangelistic success.

I walked over to Ann's driveway, and she told me her situation. She was a hospice nurse and had a ninety-year-old patient who had been in a coma for two weeks. Ann asked, "Ché, could you come with me and see this patient? I think she is going to die any minute now. Could you come and give her the last rites?"

To be honest with you, I have no idea how to give last rites. Ann comes from a Roman Catholic background, so she saw me as a priest. For her, it was a reasonable request. Wanting to be a good witness and a good neighbor, I agreed to go with her. I figured I would pray for God's hand to be upon her patient, read a passage from the Bible and that would be it.

I followed behind Ann in my car through a city north of Pasadena called Altadena. When we arrived at her client's small home, I was led to the elderly woman's room. Her name was Lois. A Philippine nurse was in attendance. I was ready to pray a simple prayer and leave when I heard the unmistakable voice of God speak to me: *I want you to raise this woman out of the coma and share the Gospel with her.*

Wow! New plan! I looked blankly at Ann and prayed silently to collect my thoughts before speaking. *Lord, You know that Sue and I have spent years reaching out to Ann and Andy through friendship evangelism, and I don't want to turn her off with what could be perceived as religious fanaticism. But I know I have heard You, Lord, and I need to obey.* So I asked Ann, "Do you mind if I pray that God would awaken her out of the coma?"

She replied, "You can do whatever you want." With that permission, I prayed for Lois to come out of her coma.

Without exaggerating, immediately after prayer, Lois came out of her coma. Not only was she awake, but her mind was sharp and crystal clear. I knew from the word the Lord had given me that she needed to hear the Gospel, so I asked about her religious background. For the next 45 minutes, she told me her whole life story. (When you are ninety years old, you have a long life story!) She told me how she had grown up as a Methodist and worked as a schoolteacher all her life, and many other details. Yet the last thing she spoke stunned me. She said, "And I knew if I died, I would go to hell. So I prayed to God: 'Keep me alive until You send someone to tell me how I can get to heaven.'"

I replied, "Lois, God has answered your prayer. He sent me to tell you how you can enter heaven." I led her in the sinner's prayer and she surrendered her life to Jesus. She ended up living for another three months on this earth, and for an eternity with Him.

As a result of seeing God miraculously bring Lois out of her coma, two other miracles occurred. First, the Philippine nurse gave her life to Jesus. And second, finally, a few months later, Ann came to one of our church services and was the first one down the aisle when I gave the altar call for salvation. She was gloriously saved and delivered.

Praying for someone in a coma might not be an everyday experience, but we can always be available to pray for those who have obvious needs. My friend Bill Johnson loves to pray for healing, and what he calls any other opportunity to "bring heaven to earth" (see Matthew 6:9–13). Along with other ideas that he offers in his incredible book *When Heaven Invades Earth*, Bill has taught his church that any person with a cast, crutches, wheelchair or obvious physical need is a natural candidate to approach with the offer of prayer. That is brilliant—and obvious. The person may say no, but many people—Christians and non-Christians alike—who have needs want prayer. It is also a great entrance to sharing testimonies and telling about the love and power of God. If the Spirit is breathing on it, it may be an hour of salvation as well.

Ask for Divine Appointments

Doing what we see the Father doing means not only speaking to those whom the Holy Spirit is telling you to address, but also being where He intends for you to be. I am sure that you have felt that impression in your gut that compels you to *go over to that table and sit* or *stand on that side of the room*. It may be a distinct impression that you should stay somewhere just a few minutes more or attend this event instead of that one, all of which may be God's way of setting up divine appointments for you. (A "divine appointment" is simply a supernatural meeting set up by God for His purposes.)

That is why hearing God's voice is so vital. He says, "My sheep listen to my voice" (John 10:27). "They will never follow a stranger" (John 10:5). There is no double-mindedness here. We were made to hear Him. So do not let the devil or anyone else tell you that you cannot.

It is interesting that before His encounter with the woman at the well Jesus "needed to go through Samaria" (John 4:4,

NKJV). Most Jews did not travel through Samaria to get from Judea to Galilee. But Jesus obviously obeyed the Father by taking that route. It yielded the divine appointment that changed a whole village.

I believe that Ann's asking me to go with her and visit Lois in her home was really a divine appointment from God, as was my venture into that wild party years ago. Larry Tomczak (who first discipled me in the Lord) wrote a book by the very title *Divine Appointments*. He encourages us to look for the ways God sets up events that may seem like coincidences but are really supernaturally planned.

You may feel a "quickening" or an urgency to do something you usually do not do. You may drive down a street you usually do not take. God may alter circumstances so that you must use a later or earlier flight or a different form of transportation. A person at work might call in sick. You might have a change of job. Someone may call your house in error. Rather than seeing these as negatives, look to see if they may be divine appointments in disguise. Then be prepared for evangelism opportunities.

It is often like being on a secret mission—and I love it. It is thrilling to think of how the Holy Spirit might be working out the details of such an encounter. It might go something like this. "Let's see: If Ché sleeps an extra half hour today after that overseas trip before going in to work, then runs into Ann getting into her car, and the appointment at his office cancels until tomorrow, then he is free to go and pray for Lois. Oh, yes. I'll want to have that other nurse at the house so she can hear the Gospel, too. Angels, ready to help? Okay, first . . ."

If we know that all of heaven rejoices when one sinner repents, perhaps heaven's hosts are ready to set up our divine appointments *if we would only ask*. This one thing I know. The Word of God says that anything we *ask* according to His will, He will do (see 1 John 5:14–15). Asking God to give you a divine appointment to share the Gospel is no doubt His favorite prayer. I cannot see Him refusing it. He says we have not because we ask not (see James 4:2). Divine appointments are for everyone, so ask. Then enjoy the process of discovery.

The bottom line is this: I believe the Holy Spirit's power is indispensable for effective evangelism. The Spirit was given for this very purpose—to bring conviction with power and a demonstration of God's love and redemption for salvation (see John 16:7–13).

Evangelism by the Spirit is the difference between that which is born of the flesh and that which is born of God. You know which is more effective! Set your heart to do what you see the Father doing, and move in power.

SECTION 5

PROFOUND EVANGELISM

15.

PROPHETIC EVANGELISM

"Woman, go and get your husband and bring him back,"
the stranger said kindly but firmly.

"I have no husband," she timidly replied.

"You are right. You have had five husbands, and the man
you are with now is not your husband."

"Sir, I see that You are a prophet," she said, stunned.

John 4:16–19, my paraphrase

The results from this brief encounter? You will recall from
our study in chapter 7 that this unbelieving woman met
the Savior, told her whole town about Him, and the entire
village was saved. Why? Because Jesus, a stranger to her,
revealed His knowledge of events in her life. She recognized
Him as a prophet, and the living waters He shared with
her at the well then became eternal life to her soul—and to
the soul of every person she brought with her.

Extraordinary evangelism? No. God's intended evangelism? Yes. One of the reasons Jesus asked His disciples to wait in Jerusalem for the intended promise of the Holy Spirit was so that they could receive power to become His witnesses (see Acts 1:4–5, 8). This power was and is manifested through the believers' use of spiritual gifts. Yes, it is possible to share the Gospel without power, but I would rather see *great fruit* that remains, such as the salvation of this whole village after one prophetic word was spoken. Personally I believe that *prophetic evangelism* is a foundation of power evangelism.

Look at this wonderful verse in Joel where the Holy Spirit is poured out on all flesh. The first gift to manifest in this outpouring is prophecy: "And afterward, I will pour out my Spirit on *all* people. Your sons and daughters will prophesy, your old men will dream dreams, your young men will see visions" (Joel 2:28, emphasis added). God loves to communicate with His people. That has been His desire since He created mankind and walked and talked with Adam and Eve in the Garden. Now, God uses you and me to speak His message of love and truth.

The Bible says to "eagerly desire spiritual gifts, especially the gift of prophecy" (1 Corinthians 14:1). Spiritual gifts are the only things we are told to covet, and prophetic gifting heads the list. Why? Because revelations given by the Holy Spirit personally and wonderfully edify other people. These utterances let them know that God is involved in their lives in a very intimate way. When you hear God call your name or speak about your unique situation, it gets your attention. If you are saved, it builds your faith and gives you hope. If you are unsaved, it may get your soul. The apostle Paul says in the same chapter of Corinthians that he wished all men prophesied; in verse 31, he says they can. It is available. It is that important and potent.

Operating in the prophetic is one of the easiest and most effective ways to move in power evangelism. If we look at verses 8 and 10 of the "spiritual gifts chapter," 1 Corinthians 12, we find three gifts from the Holy Spirit that fall into this category:

the word of wisdom—insight or counsel needed at that exact moment in a person's life;

the word of knowledge—specific illumination of a place, physical condition, name or situation known only to the person receiving the word; and

prophecy—a direct word from the heart of God to a person spoken through another about past, present or future events.

These three gifts are termed "revelational prophetic gifts." A revelational prophetic gift is one in which God discloses to you either personal information about someone else or His direction for that person, which you would have no way of knowing in the natural.

I have a friend who actually calls prophetic evangelism "cheating." She says that sharing the Gospel is so easy when God gives you insight into the person's needs that you almost cannot miss! As with the word of knowledge Jesus spoke to the woman at the well, these gifts provide astounding icebreakers that often lead to salvation.

People sometimes ask me how you know that you have received a prophetic word from God. Put simply, you feel a prophetic word in your Spirit, in your "knower." You may even feel a little uncomfortable and anxious until you are able to share it. Most often, you will hear the Lord speaking to your spirit (not in an audible voice, although some have experienced the audible voice of God). Sometimes you will "see" an impression or an incident involving the person or even see a specific word spelled out in your mind's eye.

Scripture says that by reason of *use* our senses are trained to discern good and evil (see Hebrews 5:14). It is the same with the prophetic gifts. The more you use what you are given, the more you will be trained and the easier it will become.

If you believe that the Lord is giving you a prophetic word to share, pray to hear Him clearly. When you do this, you slow down long enough to discern if what you are sensing is from the Holy Spirit and needs to be shared. Prayer also gives God a chance to work *in* us before He works *through* us. "All things by prayer and nothing without it," John Wesley once said. This is basic practice for any area of evangelism.

Are you ready? You certainly have a green light from God. It does not mean you have to "be a prophet" or be called to the five-fold ministry office of a prophet in order to prophesy. It simply means you hear the voice of God and speak it. It will change your evangelistic life forever.

Principles to Grow On

When Jesus gave the accurate word to the woman at the well, it opened her heart to believe that He was the Messiah. Because Jesus was "full of the Holy Spirit" (Luke 4:1), He was able to hear prophetically and accurately from God. Remember: *The most important prerequisite for moving in prophetic evangelism (or anything else for that matter!) is to be full of the Holy Spirit.* Here, then, are several principles that will help you move powerfully in prophetic ministry.

Walk in Obedience

Our principle of obedience, which is a theme throughout this book, is vital in prophetic evangelism. In fact, *prophetic evangelism is hearing and obeying the voice of God.* We follow His prompting and open our mouths. It is only when we speak forth the word or impression we are given to those we are evangelizing that we release the powerful witness by which souls can be saved.

It was May 2005. I was sitting on the plane waiting for takeoff from Johannesburg, South Africa, for Malawi when a large entourage arrived at the last minute. Several men boarded, dressed impeccably in Western suits, including one very distinguished man whose wife was clothed in beautiful African attire. He sat down across the aisle from me, and the flight took off.

The trip became more intriguing. As I attempted to sit unobtrusively across the aisle from the distinguished man, a "parade" began to form. One by one, people approached the man and got on their knees. They spoke briefly in their native African tongue, then rose and returned to their seats.

Finally, the parade ended, and I could resist curiosity no more. I leaned across the aisle and asked the man respectfully in English, "Pardon me. I couldn't help but notice the honor people are bestowing on you, but I am from the United States and do not know who you are. Could you please tell me?"

To my astonishment, the gentleman replied that he was the former president of Malawi, His Excellency Muluzi. He had held office for ten years, and his term ended just a year previously. He was returning home for the funeral of a former cabinet member.

We began to converse with some ease. I asked if he was a Christian—as are so many in Malawi. He replied no and explained he was a Muslim. For some reason (no doubt a word of knowledge from the Lord), I sensed the Lord prompting me to ask him if he knew or had heard of Billy Graham. He said that he had heard of him and asked me if I knew him. By God's providential grace, I had been asked to pray for and with Dr. Graham every night before his 2004 crusade in Pasadena. I could honestly say, "Yes, I know and love Billy Graham." Tactfully, I handed him

Graham's famous tract, *Peace with God*, and prayed God would use the seed.

I proceeded to tell him that I was part of a ministry bringing 56,000 dollars' worth of supplements provided by my good friends Sam and Linda Caster and their organization, MannaRelief, to donate to the AIDS orphans in Malawi and Mozambique. His attention was riveted by my comments: His wife had directed the programs for AIDS orphans during his administration! I explained to him that these supplements were powerful glyconutrients, which research was showing slowed the progression of AIDS. His Excellency Muluzi urgently wanted to know more, so he invited me to come to his home and talk with him and his wife in greater detail about the amazing Mannatech products. (The president of Mannatech and supplier of the supplements is an HIM partner.)

He gave me his phone number and told me to call and set up an appointment. Stunned, I replied that I would be delighted. My heart raced as I embraced another divine appointment from the awesome God we serve.

As the plane landed in the Malawi capital, some five thousand people were waiting to greet His Excellency Muluzi. Perhaps the richest man in Malawi, one of the very poorest nations, this man holds substantial influence. I later found out that Malawi had been at the hands of a dictator for more than thirty years before Muluzi came into office. He served as the first president under a new democracy.

On the day of my appointment with His Excellency, I arrived at a series of mansions the size of a city block. We talked for more than an hour and a half, in formal attire and presidential surroundings. We spoke in detail about helping the AIDS orphans with the Mannatech supplements.

My heart was still heavy to share Jesus further with this man. I continued to do so, whereupon, like Festus, he replied, "You have almost convinced me to believe." Yet he said he could not as his father was a Muslim, and he could not bring his family "that shame."

I asked him, "If Jesus revealed Himself in a dream to you, would you be open to it?" He replied that he would, and I asked permission to pray.

God then blew me away by putting a detailed prophetic word in my mouth that shocked His Excellency. He asked what I knew about him and his past, and I replied, "Very little, sir, except that I am to call you 'Your Excellency.'" The word had to do with his personal life and God's current call to him to further help AIDS orphans in his nation, help that would have impact on the world. It would also change how his life is recorded in history. He was stunned because he knew I had no way of knowing the details of which I spoke.

Through our talks, the love of a personal, all-knowing God had been planted in his heart. I am fervently praying for his salvation. While not currently president, Muluzi still heads the United Democratic Front in Malawi and helped hand-select the president now in office. His soul and the lives of many hang in the balance. Because of God's love for this man, the Holy Spirit's prophetic words, an obedient vessel and the saving power of Jesus Christ, a key leader and a nation could be changed. Please pray.

Step Out in Faith

Sometimes fear keeps people from moving in faith and speaking out prophetically. My conviction is that I would rather step out and be wrong than miss an opportunity to share the Gospel when the Lord is prompting me—even if it seems ridiculous. Someone once said, "You do the ridiculous and God will do the miraculous."

I was part of a ministry outreach on a college campus in Maryland when I saw a young woman coming out of the student union building. At that moment, God gave me a word of knowledge that the girl was pregnant and considering an abortion. He told me, in fact, this would be her second abortion. I quickly prayed and asked God for wisdom and grace in approaching her. Then I walked up and greeted her with kindness and explained that I was a pastor. I said, "Please don't be offended, but I sensed God telling me that you are pregnant. God loves you, and He knows you are considering an abortion. In fact, this is your second time."

The woman started crying, and through the tears she asked me how I knew. She said that she had not even told her boyfriend. Because God gave me that supernatural insight, I was able to share about God's love and salvation and His plans for her. In the end (though not immediately) both she and her boyfriend received Jesus. The two eventually became campus ministry leaders—all because of one word. Telling an unwed college student that you believe she is pregnant can definitely make you look foolish if you miss it. Yet if God has led you, sharing such a prophetic word can result in a dramatic life change as this one example shows.

Sometimes you may be wrong, but that is not the end of the world. You will not be stoned or imprisoned; God will bless you for your boldness, and you still have plenty of opportunities to be right. If you were acting in love, the one you spoke to can tell. Simply apologize and bless him or her. God uses it all for good. You may still have an opportunity to share the Gospel with the person just by virtue of your humility.

As I love to say, faith is spelled R-I-S-K, and it is faith alone that pleases God.

I remember a Thanksgiving service in 1998 in which Harriet, a Sri Lankan member of our church, brought a guest from Sri Lanka. The visitor did not come forward to receive Christ at our invitation call, but she did come up to me afterward and ask for prayer. When Harriet introduced me to her friend, she leaned over to me and whispered that her friend was not a Christian.

"So what can I do for you?" I asked.

"Please pray for me that I may have a baby. My husband and I have been married for seven years, and we have spent thousands of dollars for me to conceive, but I cannot have a baby. I even went to India recently to have a special treatment, but nothing has worked. Now my husband is ready to leave me because I cannot give him a child."

The woman was desperate and in obvious distress. I started to pray for her, asking God for the woman to conceive and have a baby. Suddenly, the Spirit of prophecy came over me, and, to my astonishment, I prophesied, "You will have a child within one year."

The moment I said those words, two things happened. First, the woman instantly collapsed onto the floor under the power of the Holy Spirit. (I had not touched her; the prophetic word released a tangible power that knocked her to the floor.) Second, I immediately wanted to take the prophecy back—not the part about having a baby; I had faith for that. I wanted to retract the specific time limit spoken that she would have a baby within one year. As a rule of thumb, I teach that when you prophesy, you should not give specific dates. The word may be true, but if the specific date is off, then the prophecy will be discredited by anyone who knows the details. But it was too late; she was out on the floor. I decided once more to be a "fool" for Christ and to trust God on the matter.

I did not see her again that Sunday, and, frankly, I forgot about this episode until the Christmas service a month later. She approached me with a beaming face, accompanied by a man I took to be her husband. Harriet, her friend from our church, also accompanied them.

"Do you remember me?" she asked.

"No, please forgive me, I don't remember," I replied.

"You prayed for me last month to get pregnant."

It came back to me. "Yes, I remember now."

"I am happy to tell you that I am three weeks pregnant!" she announced with great joy.

As a result of her miraculous pregnancy—a tangible manifestation of God's power, and certainly God's love—this woman and her husband gave their lives to Jesus that Sunday. And the next year, we had the privilege of dedicating a beautiful baby girl to the Lord in our Sunday morning service.

Release the "Spirit of Prophecy" through Testimonies

Everyone likes to hear a good story. Jesus told many parables to teach people and reach people. Our favorite kind of story always seems to be firsthand accounts of "You'll never believe what happened to me." The early Church grew rapidly as these stories of miracles, healing and salvation spread throughout the land. Whether it was the blind man declaring, "All I know is that I was blind, but now I see" (see John 9:25), or a nobleman sharing how his son, suffering hopelessly at death's door, was miraculously healed and his whole family saved (see John 4:53), the people who heard these declarations encountered a new truth. They were now confronted with the power, wonder and love of a supernatural God who *cared* and did wonders in their midst—and might do the same for them.

Bill Johnson has done much to bring back to the Body of Christ a revelation of the power of testimony. A testimony is not just a good story. Revelation 19:10 says that "the testimony of Jesus is the spirit of prophecy." As Bill explains it, whenever we share a testimony of what the power of Jesus has done—any miracle, healing, salvation account—the Spirit of prophecy is loosed over the people who are hearing it. This means the Spirit of God is actively moving on them *to create faith for the same thing to happen to them, while they are listening.* You then need only offer a time of faith-filled prayer to reap the harvest.

Thus, when you give opportunities to share testimonies of how someone just gave his heart to Jesus and it changed his life, or how she was delivered and set free from years of drug addiction and failure when she got saved, you will find the electric atmosphere of the Holy Spirit making other hearts ready to receive the same life-changing gift, just as if prophetic words were being spoken to them personally. The same is true of healing miracles. Faith comes by hearing, so faith is being built.

The Spirit of God breathes over these life-releasing words and woos those who hear. The stage is being set for power evangelism—deliverance, miracles, signs, wonders. There is an atmosphere of expectation and faith, and the Holy Spirit is hovering, ready to perform God's Word. That is also why people who hear such testimonies are often ready to receive the Lord. They are so moved by the love and compassion and power of our Savior that they cannot resist Him for themselves.

Start Prophesying!

If you want to move in prophetic evangelism, you have to start prophesying over people. You can start simply. Prophetess and author Patricia King taught me the simplest word you can give to people. She gives this prophetic word wherever she goes. She tells people that she has a word from God for them. What is the word? "Jesus loves you very much."

I spoke this word recently to an elderly waitress in a restaurant in Portland, Oregon. She happened to be by the exit as I was leaving, so I said, "I have a word from Jesus for you." She was attentive as I said, "Jesus loves you very much." At that, I walked out the door.

As I approached my rental car, the waitress ran out the door toward me. I thought perhaps I had left my credit card at the desk and she was trying to return it. But she ran up to me and said, "I want to thank you for that word. You don't know how much it meant to me."

The simplicity and the effectiveness of the prophetic amaze me. God had touched that woman's heart. Though I did not lead her to salvation "on the spot" (perhaps she was already a Christian), at the very least she was encouraged and may have received a powerful seed for salvation.

We have several people in our church who have come to know Jesus through prophetic evangelism. One of them is a precious young woman named Kayla. Here is the account of what happened to her:

> It was a very busy Friday night in mid-November. I'm a server at a nice restaurant, and almost all of my tables were taken when a new party of seven was seated in my section. They seemed very weird to me. It was as if they had never been out to eat before. Quite frankly, they were a bit annoying at the time. But dinner went on, and we built some rapport. They told me they were in town for a conference, asked my name and so on. A bit later, they asked for the check and said they had to hurry to get back to this conference they were attending. I brought the check and returned a few minutes later to cash them out. They were not ready. I came back a few minutes later, and they were still not ready. This occurred two more times—and the last time they ordered dessert! Okay, I let them enjoy dessert for a bit knowing they need to leave, and I returned for payment again. This time I told them, "Just let me know when you folks are ready."
>
> They replied, "Kayla, we have some words written down we think you need to hear."
>
> "Okaaay," I said (all the while thinking this is getting even stranger). "Let me finish up with my other tables and I will come back." All my other tables left and I returned to them.
>
> They began asking me odd questions. "Do you have a cat?"
>
> "Yes, I do," and so on and so forth. I was thinking, *What is going on here?*

Then one of them said, "We feel you have a touch of depression."

"Uh, yes," I replied. This caught my attention.

Then one woman said, "You've been searching for the truth and you've been dabbling in all sorts of things and places trying to find it." This was the turning point. Those were the truest words I'd ever heard out of someone's mouth. Just prior to this night I had decided that I had looked everywhere, and there was no truth.

I answered emphatically, "Yes!"

She replied, "Well, Kayla, Jesus is knocking at your door. God has been showing you signs your whole life and you've just been passing them by."

I stood in awe and understanding for the first time in my life. Literally a light bulb went on in my head and my heart. I know now that I was saved in that moment. I actually declared this fact to my coworkers later in my shift. I couldn't believe these words were coming out of my mouth. I didn't even know what "saved" was, but my heart knew. It has been almost one year now, and my love for truth is growing and my relationship with Jesus is the best part of my life. I have been saved from the darkness and the lies of this world. I thank God and Jesus every day for my new life.

Isn't this wonderful? Who says you cannot combine a great dinner with a little prophetic evangelism and an incredible salvation?

"Spending" Our Inheritance

As you can see, prophetic evangelism is one of the most exciting tools of power evangelism. We are so privileged to have an incredible Holy Spirit who delights in revealing hidden things for the Father's glory and for the souls of men.

Do you remember the movie a few years back about a man who stood to inherit something like eighty million dollars if he could spend that much in just one month? I don't recall much about it; actually, it sounds ridiculous. But in some ways, I see a great Kingdom parallel. Here we have a God of the miraculous giving His Son all power and authority (see Matthew 28:18). Then Jesus gives power and authority to us in His name and says we shall do even greater works than these (see John 14:12). Look at these facts: We have access to every miracle Jesus ever did—and more; the Holy Spirit is with us at *all* times; the end of the age is fast approaching; and God desires that none should perish but that the Gospel be preached to the ends of the earth (see Luke 24:47).

Let me ask you: Does God have any shortage of what He needs to get the job done? Not on His end! Quite frankly, I believe it is time to spend the inheritance. It is time to move in prophetic evangelism as the Spirit leads. Jesus paid the unfathomable price that we might access this. Let's do it. Our reward will be exponential fruit for His Kingdom and greater joy than we have ever known.

16

PRESENCE EVANGELISM

What makes us different as a people in all the earth is the *presence of God*. If we do not have His presence with us, we might as well go home. At least that is what Moses said, and I agree with him:

> "Now therefore, I pray, if I have found grace in Your sight, show me now Your way, that I may know You and that I may find grace in Your sight. And consider that this nation is Your people."
>
> And He said, "My Presence will go with you, and I will give you rest."
>
> Then he said to Him, "If Your Presence does not go with us, do not bring us up from here. For how then will it be known that Your people and I have found grace in Your sight, except You go with us? So we shall be separate, Your people and I, from all the people who are upon the face of the earth."
>
> Exodus 33:13–16, NKJV

In recent years, there has been much talk of "being in God's presence," "feeling the presence," "spending time in His presence," "moving in His presence," "being overcome by His presence" and more. While the presence of God has always been "present," I am not sure we have always been aware of it and what it means in a practical sense. I am thrilled that we are now paying attention to the presence of God in a more essential way. I believe the presence makes an unparalleled difference in our effectiveness and delight as Christians in every dimension, but especially when it comes to evangelism.

God's presence is manifested through the Holy Spirit. Or put another way, we might say that the presence *is* the Holy Spirit. Yet many people believe that encounters with the presence are reserved for special occasions that are Holy Spirit-initiated—such as when the Holy Spirit descended on Jesus at His water baptism or came as a rushing wind on those praying in the Upper Room on the day of Pentecost. The Holy Spirit (who is God) loves to be entreated to spend time with us and upon us. Remember Jesus' words to His disciples: "If I do not go away, the Helper will not come to you" (John 16:7, NKJV). And He promised that the Helper would remain with us *"forever*—the Spirit of truth, whom the world cannot receive, because it neither sees Him nor knows Him; but you know Him, for He dwells with you and will be in you" (John 14:16–17, NKJV, emphasis added).

I believe that this is the reason Jesus said we would be able to do greater things than He did: because we would be infused with the Holy Spirit and empowered by Him to do them. I like the distinction Bill Johnson makes: He says that the Holy Spirit is *within* us for our benefit, and *upon* us to help others. Many scriptural examples support this (see John 20:19–22 and Acts 2:1–4, for instance). He is *within* us when we receive Christ, and He is more powerfully at work when we are baptized with Him and learn to follow His leading. I believe we sense the Holy Spirit *upon* us when we feel His presence manifested tangibly by shaking, laughing, weeping or experiencing biblical trances, visions and dreams. He can also be upon us when we are caught up in worship, unaware of time, in the presence of angels, deep in prayer or repentance, or lost in a corporate move of God.

It is the "upon us" or the overshadowing aspect that this chapter will mainly address. I call this *presence evangelism*. Immediately, two powerful scriptural examples come to mind when I think of the Holy Spirit coming "upon" someone in an amazing way: (1) when the Holy Spirit overshadowed Mary to conceive Jesus (see Luke 1:35), and (2) when the Spirit knocked the unsaved Paul to the ground, resulting in his conversion and history-making future (see Acts 9).

Encounter with His Presence

Let me share a contemporary story with you about the power of this special kind of evangelism. I am humbled by this means through which God arrests hearts for the Kingdom.

This is Lisa's story. Lisa was a rebellious fifteen-year-old crack addict who was wasting away on drugs and gang activity in the Las Vegas area; she had been shot at twice. Lisa's mother, at her wit's end, shipped Lisa off to live with her aunt in Seattle, hoping things might improve.

On a visit to Pasadena, this aunt brought Lisa, a Korean American, to a small group ministry I was holding for Korean Christians. She had shared with me Lisa's plight, but one look at Lisa told it all. She was dressed in baggy, gang-style clothes; her face was hardened and dark. She certainly did not look fifteen; she looked like a burned-out adult.

All during my message, I could not help but focus on Lisa. I hoped she would answer the altar call. No such response.

We moved into a time of ministry, and I prayed for people to be filled with the Holy Spirit. Several people fell to the floor and "manifested" God's presence by shaking or trembling. I could not help but wonder what thoughts were going through Lisa's mind during all of this. I decided to ask her.

I introduced myself and chatted with Lisa for a few moments. I asked her if she would like to give her life to Jesus, but she said she was not ready yet. I appreciated her honesty and told her so. Then I asked if she would mind if I just prayed for her instead.

She looked at me and replied indifferently, "Do whatever you want." She seemed bored and ready to leave as soon as possible. I felt I should give her a little space and stood several feet away. Then I quietly said these words: "Jesus, please reveal to Lisa how much You love her."

No sooner had the words left my mouth than Lisa started to laugh. I could tell she was trying not to laugh because of her unsuccessful attempts to cover her mouth with her hands. Now I knew the Holy Spirit was flooding her.

I told Lisa not to fight the laughter. I explained that the Holy Spirit was revealing Himself to her—and that was a good thing. (Many people call the recent renewal the "laughing revival" because people often laugh uncontrollably when the Holy Spirit fills them with unspeakable joy.)

At this point, I moved near her to bless what the Father was doing and to ask for more for her. As soon as I lifted my hands over her, she fell to the floor speaking in tongues. This amazed me. I had not led her to the Lord, nor had we prayed the sinner's prayer together. In fact, she had just told me she was not ready to come to Christ.

I asked the Lord to give me Scripture concerning what I was witnessing, and Acts 10 came immediately to my mind: As Peter was preaching to the house of Cornelius, the Holy Spirit fell, and the members of the household all began to speak in tongues.

Apparently Lisa had changed her mind about salvation when she experienced that initial touch of the Spirit in laughter. She was then converted and filled with the Holy Spirit at the same time.

Lisa stayed on the floor for almost two hours. (This is not uncommon at meetings where people are enjoying the presence of the Holy Spirit.) She continued speaking in tongues and shaking under the power of the Spirit.

Nearly everyone was leaving, so I went over to her and told her it was time to go. She said in reply: "I can't move. I can't get up. There are too many . . . too many."

I thought she meant that she was seeing too many demons; I figured I would have another late night ahead ministering deliverance.

"There are too many what?" I asked.

"Too many faces," she answered.

"Faces of whom?"

"Faces of my friends. Their faces have been flashing before me all night," she said. Her answer hit me with tremendous force. God had been showing her the faces of her unsaved gang-member friends who were going to hell.

With His kind presence enveloping her that night, God not only saved her precious soul and filled her with His Spirit, but He also filled her heart with prayers for the salvation of her gang-member friends. She stayed on the floor unable to move for the next eight hours, compelled to intercede through resting in the presence of God. Her life was radically changed forever . . . and, no doubt, so were the lives of those for whom she prayed.

Be a "Conduit"

In Jesus' famous prayer to teach us, He said simply to the Father, "Thy kingdom come, Thy will be done in earth, as it is in heaven" (Matthew 6:10, KJV). Literally translated, this is in the imperative or command form. It reads: "Come, Thy Kingdom. Be done, Thy will." There is no gray area. Jesus was telling us that the way it is in heaven is what we are to pray for on earth.

Bill Johnson says that we are "conduits" of heaven. I particularly like this because it takes the focus off of us and gives God His rightful place and glory. A conduit is merely a channel to allow (or attract) something to flow through it to something else—such as an electrical conduit or a water conduit. Someone told me that pure gold makes the best electrical conduit because there are no impurities to slow the process. That is an interesting parallel for us. If we are conduits, we can be "clear channels" for the presence of God wherever we go, and things will change.

These suggestions that follow will lead you not only to continuous intimacy with God but also to continuous awareness of His presence in you and upon you. This will help you bring God's powerful presence into your evangelism encounters, and keep you filled with His joy and strength for the journey.

Listen to Worship Music

Worship music brings us into intimacy with God and lifts us out of the everyday realm and into the realm of heaven. Through listening and joining in praise, we can be filled afresh with hope, the goodness of God, the reality and majesty of His Kingdom and His love for us. Our hearts can be softened where they have grown hard. We are enabled to give our offering of love to Him. The Bible tells us that He inhabits the praises of His people (see Psalm 22:3, KJV). Is that presence? Yes! I especially encourage you to do this in the privacy of your own home or in special "worship only" meetings where there is time for the unique presence of God to inhabit your heart.

Commune with God

Someone once said, "Talking *about* God is not the same as talking *to* God." There is nothing that can replace intimate communion with God. Whether it is a walk in the woods or a quiet moment on your sofa, as the psalmist David said, we must pour out our hearts before God (see Psalm 62:8) and share our deepest hopes, wants, desires and fears. It is a privilege to spend time thanking God for who He is and what He has done in our lives, and for the incredible sacrifice Jesus made for us. It is good to express our amazement and satisfaction with the Holy Spirit's work in us and others, and to recount the blessings of God.

Listen

Sometimes we are too busy talking to God to realize that He wants to talk to us. In fact, He usually wants to speak to us more than we want to listen to Him. Give Him a chance. Sitting quietly yields amazing results. No one likes a one-way conversation, including God. Psalm 25:14 says that God will make known the secret things to those He loves. If you have never heard any of His secrets, perhaps He has not had the chance to tell you. One secret is that He loves you incredibly, and is excited about your heart to please Him. Another secret is that the Lord loves to envelop you in His presence while He is speaking. You will have to let the Holy Spirit come and settle upon you to find out the rest.

Use Soaking Prayer

Perhaps you have heard the term "soaking" in Christian circles in recent years. The concept refers to peaceful resting in the Lord's presence; it is a time for "filling up" with the Holy Spirit (see Ephesians 5:18). Soaking prayer is not a "quick

181

pass through the prayer line." One way it occurs is when fellow believers spend time being a gentle conduit of the Holy Spirit for you. Usually this involves laying on of hands or perhaps a gentle touch on the forehead or shoulder. It is somewhat like receiving a "transfusion" of God's presence and usually leaves you refreshed and renewed. Many people in past years have gone (and still do go) to "watering holes" known for soaking prayer—such as Toronto or Pasadena and Redding in California. Soaking prayer is happening in countless local churches and cell groups all over the nation and the globe.

Soaking prayer can also be a private experience. You can soak as you spend time alone in God's presence at home or somewhere else. You find yourself just lying or sitting in His presence for extended lengths of time and flowing with what the Holy Spirit is doing in you and through you. These are usually times that the Holy Spirit simply chooses to touch you in a special way. Many people find their hearts getting healed; their bodies being healed; joy returning; depression leaving; or, as in Lisa's case, salvation followed by intercession for the lost.

Presence evangelism gives the expression "Go with God" a whole new meaning. When God's sovereign presence is upon you, when the Holy Spirit overshadows you, there are no limits to what may happen. That is why it is so incredible.

May we crave His presence increasingly and take it to a dying world. May we be so infused with Him, such a conduit for Him, that people are forever changed wherever we go. May others see Him and sense Him in us, and desire His great salvation.

SECTION 6

PURPOSEFUL EVANGELISM

17

NEW APOSTOLIC
WINESKINS

What are apostolic wineskins? And why a chapter on them in the middle of a book on evangelism? We have purposed in this book to understand and "do only what [we see the] Father doing" (John 5:19). We have seen that He is doing something marvelous as the greatest harvest ever known begins to pour in across the globe. There must be containers for this phenomenal end-time harvest, and that is where the new wineskins come in.

I feel that it is important to look at what the Father is doing toward that end around the nation and the world— the movement that is swelling is unlike anything the Church has seen before. Perhaps as you read this chapter you will sense a quickening in your spirit that your call to evangelism could take you farther than you ever expected. This is exactly what happened to me.

When I was a young believer, I heard a statement that profoundly influenced my life. Arthur Wallis said: "If you want to do what is best for your life, find out what God is doing in your generation and give yourself to it." I made a commitment in my heart to do just that. It was about that same time that my father made me a job offer in the ministry. He was the first Korean Southern Baptist pastor in North America and planted a church in Washington, D.C., in 1958. It was now the mid-70s, and he was asking me to be his youth pastor.

The honorable thing would be to say yes. I was already volunteering with the youths at the church and speaking to them on Sundays. Yet I was also involved with a community of believers meeting in my best friend's apartment on Saturday nights. It was Larry Tomczak's vision to establish a "new wineskin" church. Larry told me that he could not offer me a full-time position, although I had a strong desire to be in full-time vocational ministry. But he assured me that if I was faithful and grew in character, God would raise me up to that calling.

I had a choice to make. I could continue with church life as I had always known it—that is, become a paid staff member of a denominational church—or take a leap of faith and serve as a believer in a new church plant. What Arthur Wallis had said made my decision easy. I had to be on the cutting edge of what God was doing.

The hard part was explaining this to my father. He told me that as a Korean, I had to serve the Korean people. But I countered by saying (and it was more of a prophecy than an explanation): "Dad, I believe that I will be able to do more to serve the Korean people in the future if I am trained by Larry in this new church." Little did I know that I would be leading a network of apostolic churches in Korea some twenty years later. My father knew Larry and he wanted me to be trained, so he blessed me to go.

I look back and see the sovereign hand of God on my life. Not only did that small group of people meeting in Larry's apartment on Saturday nights grow into a church that now has more than three thousand members, but out of it many churches have been planted. It was, in fact, basically an Apostolic Network before its time. (I will define this idea of networks further as we go along.) I became an ordained pastor during that time, and oversaw eight churches. Although Larry and I are no longer a part of that particular network, I received tremendous training for what the Lord had planned for me: leading my own network and coming into all that is still unfolding before me today.

We are living in the most exciting period of Church history. I have often heard Peter Wagner say that more people have come to know Jesus Christ in the last fifty years than all other centuries combined. He maintains that the Church worldwide is coming into the "Second Apostolic Age." To retain this massive harvest, God is establishing new wineskins (see Matthew 9:14–17). It reminds me of a verse from the book of Isaiah. God confronts His people by saying: "See, I am doing a new thing! Now it springs up; do you not perceive it?" (Isaiah 43:19).

I see these new wineskins as alliances of those knit by common goals in the Spirit and formed, as I put it, by the same "spiritual DNA." This is powerful and holy, and not of man's doing. That is why it is so thrilling to me. Jesus promised that "of the increase of his government and peace there will be no end" (Isaiah 9:7). The Lord is establishing His powerful, ruling Bride in the earth. I am confident we are seeing this come to pass right before our eyes.

These alliances, or networks, go by different names. Some terms you might hear are *ChurchNext*, *Postdenominational churches*, the *Third Day church*, *new churches*, the *House Church Movement* and *Apostolic Networks*. I chose to label this wave of alliances as *Apostolic Networks*. *Apostolic* because there is a recognized "apostle," an apostolic leader, who is heading each network, and *networks* because these moves of the Spirit have either planted churches or joined with existing churches to further the Kingdom of God. What

187

is important, of course, is not which term we use, but that we recognize that God is indeed doing a new thing.

Because these groups of churches and individuals carry the same vision, they move together easily and multiply. As the Word of God says, "Can two walk together, unless they are agreed?" (Amos 3:3, NKJV). Churches seem to grow quickly in these networks and the outcome is synergistic. There is more power in their combined spiritual and natural resources than if they remained separate. Just as Scripture talks about "one man [chasing] a thousand, or two [putting] ten thousand to flight" (Deuteronomy 32:30), I see spiritual power being released tenfold in such networks in every aspect of the Kingdom of God.

I firmly believe that such networking with its exponential power is the means by which many of the prophetic words spoken to the Body of Christ will come to pass. Time after time, we are hearing how God is speeding up the fulfillment of His Word. What took many years will now take few; what took months will now take weeks; what took weeks will now take days. When I read a Scripture like the one that asks, "Can a country be born in a day?" (Isaiah 66:8), I know that "church as usual" cannot be the means by which widespread salvation will be accomplished. Man-made kingdoms and boundary-conscious churches will never accomplish these goals. It will take signs, wonders and miracles, the pouring out of His Spirit upon all flesh, and the Kingdom of God being the priority of His people. I am convinced these new apostolic movements are a part of that solution.

David Barrett is one of the most renowned and respected statisticians of matters regarding the Christian Church. He has stated that this New Apostolic Reformation is the largest and fastest-growing segment of evangelical Christianity in the world today. Peter Wagner explains in his book *Changing Church* (Regal, 2004), an outstanding source of information on these new apostolic churches, how Barrett has divided world Christianity numerically into six "megablocs." The largest megabloc comprises Roman Catholics; second in number is this New Apostolic Reformation—it is larger than the Protestant and Orthodox megablocs, for instance, and growing faster.

Clearly, the Holy Spirit is breathing on this new thing. I believe if one wants to be an effective church planter or be part of a church that is moving with the purposes of God, one will be actively involved in these new apostolic churches. Of course, the Holy Spirit may be leading you otherwise. But as a general principle of success, you want to go where God is moving and not just ask God to bless what you are doing or what you want to do or what someone else has done in the past.

I learned this by experience.

During a time of transition in my ministry, God called me out of a wineskin network that I had been part of for many years. I then fully intended to join a different network that was reaching the nations, planting churches and moving in power and love. Through a series of events and a clear prophetic word from Cindy Jacobs, however, God called me to father my own network, something that had not entered my mind. I obeyed, and Harvest International Ministry was launched in October 1996. If I had simply asked God to bless my own plans, I would probably have missed this ministry opportunity.

Let me add that the reason we grew so fast in fewer than ten years is because we are a "network of networks." Here is a small sampling of how this works. Paul Tan, a member of our HIM apostolic team, also leads a network called "City Blessing Churches" that reaches Indonesians around the world. Likewise, HIM member Terry Edwards oversees a network of churches in the Philippines and in Northern California. He has planted many of these churches with his apostolic team. David Prakasam heads more than 450 churches in India, and his brother-in-law, Minovah

Nickelson, leads some sixty churches. There are so many wonderful HIM people and ministries I could mention. What is most important is that we are doing what we see the Father doing around the world, and He is blessing our work.

Not only are we planting churches, but we are also involved with transforming society and ministering to the poor. This includes children at risk and AIDS orphans in Africa, as I mentioned earlier. At this writing, we are sponsoring nine orphanages around the world. We have established a soymilk factory in North Korea that is producing and feeding seven thousand children every day. We have trained thousands of pastors from America to India to Africa. We have helped with disaster relief through our overseas churches as they reach out to victims of tsunamis and famine. What we can do together far exceeds anything we could do by ourselves. Listening to the Holy Spirit enables us to act more quickly than if we followed the timetables and plans of man.

I am amazed at God's grace because "the LORD has done this, and it is marvelous in our eyes" (Psalm 118:23). We simply jumped into the river of God and allowed the Holy Spirit to lead us and establish the work of our hands. All glory and honor to Jesus! I believe we are just getting started.

Yet we are only one network of thousands that are springing up all over the world. I have mentioned my friends Rolland and Heidi Baker and Iris Ministries in Africa and other nations. John and Carol Arnott lead an apostolic network called Partners in Harvest. Rick Joyner leads the Morningstar Churches. Rice Brooks leads the Every Nation network. Bill Hamon leads Christian International Churches. These are just a few of the many Apostolic Networks in North America. Apostolic Networks are springing up in Brazil, Nigeria, India, Indonesia and, of course, China, with its House Church Movement. More than 150 million Chinese people are involved in the explosive growth of Christianity that is contained in these new house-church wineskins.

More wineskins are going to be needed; church planting is the answer. We will discuss church planting in the chapter that follows. Please note that I am all for denominations planting churches. We need to plant as many churches as we can. Yet I firmly believe in the principle of "life before structure." We can plant "stillborn" churches born of man and find no life. If we plant churches that are in conjunction with the way that God is moving today, I believe we will see greater Kingdom success. That is my heart's desire: to please the King. Let's continue now with the most effective plan for helping to bring in this marvelous harvest.

18

CHURCH PLANTING

The single most effective evangelistic methodology is planting churches.

C. Peter Wagner

This revolutionary observation had a profound impact on me from the moment I first heard it years ago as a student attending one of Dr. Wagner's classes at Fuller Theological Seminary.

Having come to see the truth of this incredible observation firsthand, I believe that any comprehensive work on evangelism is incomplete without addressing the magnificent relationship between leading people to Christ and church planting. We learned in the last chapter that church planting is an important means of providing new wineskins to "contain" the harvest. It is also, in an interesting twist, an awesome (yet quite overlooked) tool for motivating church leaders and church members to go out and win those souls for Jesus. Planting a church is a hands-on adventure with a definable goal—one that compels all involved in a way nothing else can.

I give you in this chapter ten reasons why church planting and evangelism are so complimentary, so fulfilling and so effective for all members of the Body of Christ, and why I believe church planting is the best method of evangelizing the *world*.

Church Planting Is a Biblical Model

Paul and his apostolic team changed the known world of their day through aggressive and Spirit-led church planting. In *Church Planting for a Great Harvest* (Regal, 1990), Peter Wagner states,

> Church planting is the New Testament way of extending the Gospel. Trace the expansion of the Church through Jerusalem, Judea, Samaria, and the uttermost parts of the earth and you will see that church planters led the way. This is a Kingdom activity strongly endorsed by God our King. Collectively, as a community of the Kingdom, we can scarcely feel that we are obeying God if we fail to plant churches and plant them intentionally and aggressively.

As an example of this from modern Church history, consider the Methodist "circuit riders." More than two hundred years ago, these itinerant preachers traveled by horseback from town to town, holding revival meetings throughout the Eastern United States. Church planting was their God-directed goal, and Methodist churches sprang up in nearly every rural area where their evangelistic meetings were held.

Church Planting Serves the Community

All communities have numerous needs, especially the inner cities of America. I have gone into South Central Los Angeles and preached the Gospel. People were saved. Yet bringing people to salvation is only a part of fulfilling the Great Commission. As we saw earlier, we have to engage in servant evangelism. The poor have to be fed. The drug addicts need to be delivered and rehabilitated. People need to be educated and helped to find housing and jobs and practical resources. Through planting local churches with a vision that fits the needs of the people within the area, we can best address their requirements, and make a more powerful impact on our cities and communities. We need to plant hundreds of churches with this type of holistic vision in all of our cities.

I talked with an executive of a Christian social service organization that is involved primarily with feeding the poor. I was curious to know what he considered the best way of obeying Jesus' directive to help the poor. I was amazed when he said that the best way to do this is to plant churches.

It is interesting to me (but not surprising) that after Hurricanes Katrina and Rita devastated the southern United States gulf states in 2005, some of the most effective relief, relocation and feeding efforts for the thousands and thousands of displaced people came through churches. Even in a city as far away as Los Angeles, an Assemblies of God church called the Dream Center took in more than three hundred evacuees from the central gulf storms. I believe church intervention will be even more strategic in the days ahead as Christ's return nears. Father God always intended for His Church to be the light in days of darkness and disaster. He never intended for any government to meet every need—but rather for people to have to turn to the one and only true God and His people in that crucial hour.

I believe that God will show His glory through the Church in days ahead in just this manner, and that the establishment of effective local churches is more important than ever before. We found the same to be true as our Harvest International Ministry churches joined to send aid administered through our local network churches in southern India after the ravaging tsunami of 2004 in that area. Our churches closest to the cities and villages hardest hit were on hand to help feed and clothe the victims and to share the love of Christ and the Gospel, and as a result, new churches are still being birthed. The same thing happened after the astonishing earthquake in Pakistan in 2005. Our apostle who oversees 200 churches in Pakistan, Shahbaz Bhatti, was able to bring relief to thousands of victims quickly as HIM partnered with him with financial donations.

Church Planting Releases New Leaders

Unknown numbers of quality leaders and ministers in the Body of Christ are atrophying because there is no challenging ministry for them in the local church. Their gifts are not being fully utilized. They have been cell or home group leaders for years, but they need to graduate to church planting. Yet, because their pastors do not want to lose them, these individuals are held back when the Kingdom could be expanded.

This restraint of leaders blocks growth all the way down the line: Other people beneath them have less opportunity to move up in ministry. I believe the whole church body suffers when its leaders are not released into service.

Many years ago, Larry Tomczak came to me and said that we had too many pastors on the staff. He asked me if I was willing to be sent out to plant a church. He did not know that God had spoken to me earlier with a message that I was to go to Los Angeles and plant a church. I was longing for this, but had no idea how the release would ever come. I wonder how many pastors and lay people are longing for their church or denomination to send them out. I can hear God saying again, "Let My people go."

Church Planting Opens Ministry Opportunities

There is nothing like on-the-job training. You can go to seminary, you can read a book, you can talk about it with friends, but the best way to learn about the realities and demands of church life and ministry is to plant a church. It is amazing what happens when you step out of the boat. Some things are better than you had imagined, and some things are far more challenging. I know I grew far more in character and experience through the planting of two churches than in the whole of my Christian life before I began. Church planting is one of the most difficult things you can do in ministry. Yet it is one of the most fulfilling. I have no regrets because I feel I grew by light-years as a result of these experiences.

And this is true of everyone who is involved in helping plant the new church. Many people who could not hold positions in the church from which they were sent (because they were already filled) can now be trained in these areas. There is now room for everyone to help in new ways— from teaching new member classes to following up with visitors, creating structure for the children's ministry, overseeing outreach and member care, supporting the music ministry, getting involved in home-group leadership and more. As they rise to leadership positions, they can then train others to replace them. That is healthy growth and reproduction.

Church Planting Creates New Wineskins for the New Wine

I believe God is always moving. He is pouring out His Spirit in new ways. He has more of a desire to reach the lost than we do. Yet each city and community and people you want to reach pose new challenges. As I shared in the previous chapter, we need to recognize that God is establishing a new wineskin: apostolic churches. These churches must be flexible and willing to adjust readily to what the Father is saying. What the Father is saying to one urban area about the destiny and call of that place may be completely different from His message to another area. The kind of manifestation the Holy Spirit chooses in one place may not be the same as another. (Examples of this include laughter in Toronto, teeth being filled with gold in South America, mass salvation and church planting among the poor in Mozambique, even the growth of unusually large vegetables in some areas of the world where revival has been.)

New churches that are planted have the advantage of being flexible or "current." They are not forced to stay within the confines of prior traditions or of any "baggage" that could hinder them from doing the new thing that God might be saying. This is not to say, of course, that the older or established churches in an area are wrong. For that matter, a new church can be inflexible. But there are times and moves of God when He is looking for churches that are willing to take ministry "outside the box" and follow His leading, and not stay in the usual comfort zones. Generally new wineskins are a good fit for this new wine.

Church Planting Can Reach a New Generation

Many existing churches will not be able to reach the upcoming generation. How many churches do you know of the boomer generation that really embrace the tattoos, nose rings, belly-button rings, wild hair and hip-hop music of that generation? As Peter Wagner posits in *Church Planting for a Great Harvest*, "One of the immediate implications of rapid culture change is that many members of the new generation will not be won to Christ in their parents' church." To the new generation, their parents' music is outdated, the messages are irrelevant and the reception is not warm. This is why I am involved with a team of leaders (under HIM) to plant new apostolic churches on major college campuses and elsewhere so that we can effectively reach the next generation.

Church Planting Reaches All Types of People

"Are we in America prepared for the fact that most non-Christians yet to be won to Christ will not fit readily into the kinds of churches we now have?" This question, quoted in Jim Peterson's *Evangelism as a Lifestyle* (NavPress, 1980), was posed by Ralph Winter, a friend and missions expert who founded the United States Center for World Missions in Pasadena, California.

Just as there are no one-size-fits-all shoes, there is not one kind of church that meets the needs of all kinds of people. Likewise, churches are living organisms that grow and change just as people grow and change; the process is ongoing. New churches are a part of that process.

Furthermore, our awe-inspiring God has great delight in diversity. He loves every kind of person, every kind of tongue, tribe and nation. He celebrates cultural differences and preferences just as He values individual differences. If God would go to the lengths of making every single snowflake unique—even the masses of them in the Arctic that no living being will ever see—how much more is He concerned with delighting each creative being He has made in His image? We need different churches to reach different people. Old, young, teens, middle-aged, quiet, loud, shy, overt, bikers, hikers, bakers or bookworms, God wants a place for everyone in His family. As one friend says, we need lots of "flavors" to reflect a really big God.

Church Planting Commissions "Nationals"

I strongly believe that anyone desiring to plant churches should consider planting new apostolic cross-cultural churches in the United States. This means intentionally including internationals or people from other cultures in your church membership. By reaching internationals or bicultural people on our own turf, we potentially have leaders who can be sent out as church planters in their home countries. These kinds of leaders are referred to as "nationals." It is a well-established fact that nationals and indigenous leaders have a better success rate with churches among their own people than do outsiders attempting to do the same work.

It is amazing to consider what can happen when we evangelize international students who come to the United States to obtain graduate degrees. It has been shown that within 25 years, 75 percent of these brilliant people will become leaders in their own nations. Thus, bringing these students to Jesus and laying the foundation of Christianity in their lives while they are in our nation means we can have far-reaching impact on their nations that might never happen under other conditions. Planting cross-cultural churches is powerful.

Since 1977, I have had a tremendous burden for China. For years I have been reaching out to the Chinese in Los Angeles and incorporating them into our church as the Lord leads. These brothers and sisters are preparing to go to mainland China and plant churches as God opens the door. The truth is that we are intentionally building a multicultural church in order to reach the nations. At one count, there were more than 43 nations represented in our congregation at Harvest Rock Church in the greater Los Angeles area.

Church Planting Fosters Racial Reconciliation

I once heard Billy Graham say that racism is the number one problem in the world. Racial reconciliation must begin in the Church. We cannot expect the world to bring about reconciliation in a humanistic way because racism is a spiritual problem. The Church has the solution to this problem through Jesus and His unconditional love. Only He can fill our hearts and deliver us from prejudice. By planting churches in other cultures, we have a chance to bless that culture spiritually and practically. It would be wonderful if the Korean churches would use their resources to plant churches among the African Americans in any given city. It would be great to see African Americans plant churches among the Hispanics, and so on. This breaks stereotypes and hatred, and models an example for the community. It crosses the boundaries of self-imposed segregation.

The blessing that will be called forth upon those who are willing to initiate the Christlike step to bless and restore will be no small thing, and I believe it will have eternal repercussions. Such restoration and reconciliation is a priority of the Father's heart. "How good and how pleasant it is for brethren to *dwell* together in unity! . . . For there the LORD *commanded* the blessing—life forevermore" (Psalm 133:1, 3, NKJV, emphasis added). *Dwelling* together connotes *abiding*—not a "flyby" at the annual multi-church picnic!

Church Planting Can Be Your Most Fulfilling Cause

Coming from me, you might take this as far too subjective a statement. Yet because I really believe that planting churches is the most effective way of evangelizing the lost, I have committed my life to seeing churches planted. I do not have to plant them myself, but I desire to help those who do in any way possible. And I can honestly say this is one of the most exciting and fulfilling ministry experiences of my life. It perhaps is only exceeded by the joy of leading someone to Jesus Christ and knowing that one life is changed forever.

So as not to sound biased, I would like you to hear someone else's words about the thrill of the church plant. This is from Aubrey Malphurs in *Planting Growing Churches* (Baker, 1992):

> Starting a church is one of the most exciting spiritual ventures a group of Christians may ever undertake. There are several factors behind this intense excitement. One is that church planting appeals to the pioneer spirit within most people. The idea of starting something new and different appeals to a spirit of entrepreneurship that lies deep within the souls of many of us. We relish the idea of being on the cutting edge of something new! Another factor is the sense of anticipation. As Christians we know that God is capable of doing extraordinary things in and through our lives such as building a great church. While we may never have experienced these things personally, we're aware that others have. But maybe it's our turn! Maybe God is about to do something extraordinary, and we're going to be part of it. A third factor is expectation. Not only do we anticipate that God could do something special through the new church, but deep within our beings we expect Him to do so. We can feel it in our bones! We sense that the time is right, and that time is now! Life is too short, and we don't have many opportunities to be involved in something special for God. Consequently, let's step out in faith and be part of a great new work for God.

May these ten insights breathe fire upon those of you who have dreams in your hearts of planting churches. May it engender desire in those of you who are called to supportive roles in a church-planting team. And whatever your call, may you be inspired to know the importance of your position in the local church and your call to help build the Kingdom.

Now let's discover how to take that call to the one corner of the world where you can have unparalleled influence for good: your workplace. Does the "sacred" really have a place in a "secular" setting? Let's find out.

19

WORKPLACE EVANGELISM

One of the hottest subjects in the Church today has to do with workplace or marketplace ministry. Here is what some of the leaders in the Church are saying:

- Franklin Graham: "God has begun an evangelism movement in the workplace that has the potential to transform our society."
- Peter Wagner: "I believe the workplace movement has the potential to impact society as much as the Reformation."

Society is taking notice. You can see a significant trend through what secular business magazines are saying. *Business Week* reported in November 2001 that more than ten thousand Bible and prayer groups were meeting in the workplace. *Fortune* magazine did a cover story in July 2001 about believers getting organized in their desire to bridge spirituality and work. I believe that the momentum has only increased.

We are also seeing the changes in corporate America. Coca-Cola Christian Fellowship, located at Coca-Cola's corporate world headquarters in Atlanta, Georgia, has more than 275 people who attend a Bible study. American Airlines, Sears and Intel all have prayer meetings and Bible studies. Sears even has its own company-sponsored choir and has produced a professionally recorded CD.

What is going on?

A major shift is taking place in the workplace. This is happening because the Church is going through two theological paradigm shifts. First, the Church is recognizing that the Church in the workplace *is* the Church. Peter Wagner helps by clarifying different uses of the word *church*. He uses the sociological term "nuclear church" for the assembly that typically meets on Sundays in a "church building." The "extended church" is Christians *as* the Church in the workplace the rest of the week. In other words, the Church is the *people* of God and not a building.

The second theological shift is the understanding that *all* believers are ministers. The hierarchical distinction that only the paid leaders of a church are its ministers evolved during Constantine's era in the fourth century. It was never God's idea.

Ephesians is very clear about this:

And He Himself gave some to be apostles, some prophets, some evangelists, and some pastors and teachers, for the equipping of the *saints for the work of ministry,* for the edifying of the body of Christ, till we all come to the unity of the faith and of the knowledge of the Son of God, to a perfect man [*mature,* NIV], to the measure of the stature of the fullness of Christ; that we should no longer be children, tossed to and fro and carried about with every wind of doctrine, by the trickery of men, in the cunning craftiness of deceitful plotting, but, speaking the truth in love, may grow up in all things into Him who is the head—Christ—from whom the whole body, joined and knit together by what every joint supplies, *according*

to the effective working by which every part does its share, causes
growth of the body for the edifying of itself in love.

Ephesians 4:11–16, NKJV, emphasis added

The Church is beginning to understand that every believer
is a priest (see 1 Peter 2:9). Every believer is a minister. When
you are called to the workplace and anointed by God to serve
in your field of work, you are doing ministry.

Pastor Dick Bernal of San Jose, California, told a story at
one of our conferences about meeting a successful doctor
who had given up his practice. The doctor felt that he could
not serve God unless he was in full-time ministry as a "paid
vocational pastor," so he quit his job and started a church.
His church was struggling. Dick spoke to the doctor and
straightened out his thinking. He helped him understand
that practicing medicine *was* a ministry, and that he could
best serve God by serving people with the gifts and education
for which God had anointed him. When he returned to his
medical practice, he started to flourish in his desire to serve
God. He now understood and put into practice the fact that
he was a doctor whose ministry was *in* the workplace.

I think of it this way: Both what you do in the workplace
and what you bring to it are ministry. In the doctor's case,
practicing medicine is a ministry in itself. If he also prays
with his patients or shares the Gospel with them, that is also
ministry—the ministry of evangelism.

When you think about it, most people are not called to
vocational nuclear-church ministry. I have heard that only 1
percent of Christians are in vocational nuclear-church service.
That means that 99 percent of the Church will spend 60 to 70
percent of their lives in the *workplace* doing ministry. We need
to *empower* and *equip* that 99 percent to bring transformation
to the workplace.

Unfortunately, the Church has been duped into making
a distinction between its place in the "secular" and the
"sacred." This flows from centuries of Greek thinking that

separates the "less spiritual" workplace from the Church. This, too, is an imposed thinking from which the Church is only now beginning to recover. I like what author Dallas Willard says: "There is truly no division between sacred and secular except what we have created."

I also like to put this in context with what Jesus said in a prayer to His Father:

> "But now I come to You, and these things I speak in the world, that they may have My joy fulfilled in themselves. I have given them Your word; and the world has hated them because they are not of the world, just as I am not of the world. I do not pray that You should take them out of the world, but that You should keep them from the evil one. They are not of the world, just as I am not of the world. . . . As You sent Me *into* the world, I also have sent them *into* the world. . . . I do not pray for these alone, but also for those who will believe in Me *through their word*."
>
> John 17:13–16, 18, 20, NKJV, emphasis added

I see three important principles in this passage: (1) We will find *His joy fulfilled in us* as we are involved in *reaching the world*; (2) Jesus always intended for us to be *in* the world and not hiding from it; and (3) He actually sent us into the world and is *expecting* us to lead many to believe on Him *through our word*.

Too many people have the wrong impression that there is something magical about the paid vocational ministry. They believe that it somehow increases the "value" of one person's lifework over that of someone else who is paid by other employment. It is not the source of pay that determines your effectiveness in life or in sharing the Gospel: It is your commitment to Christ, your message and your anointing.

I identify four types of Christians in the workplace. The first is the Christian who goes to work and has no impact. He does not understand his high calling as a minister at work. The second is the Christian who lives by Christian principles in the workplace, and might at least be noticed for his values. The third is the believer who is living by the power of the Holy Spirit in his work life and is looking to evangelize and share his faith. The fourth type is the Christian who is committed to transforming the workplace and taking dominion for Christ.

Dismiss right now any notion that you are not a full-time minister for Jesus Christ and enjoy the blessings of serving Him in evangelism or any other ministry if you are working in the marketplace.

Let me give you a few examples of effective evangelism in the workplace—by workplace ministers on their job.

A computer consultant's marriage was crumbling. His Christian coworker counseled him, and his marriage was restored. As a result, the man gave his heart to Jesus. He eventually contributed more than one million dollars to support the church he then joined. These two men formed a Bible study at their company, and the company's president attended the meetings.

A teacher led his seventh-grade student to Christ after sharing a testimony in class about experiencing heaven. The girl approached her teacher later, saying that she felt the presence of God for the first time ever.

An executive staff member of a United States senator on Capitol Hill shared the Gospel faithfully with the senator (who was half Jewish) during her tenure on his personal staff.

A nurse prayed for one of her critically ill patients and led her to the Lord on her deathbed.

A private businessman doing trade in mainland China uses his warehouse there to offer undercover Bible studies for his unsaved workers.

A truck driver is sharing the Gospel at truck stops all across the country.

An executive in Texas holds large monthly "power lunches" for unsaved businessmen and women and has well-known speakers from every walk of life—astronauts, sports figures, politicians, authors, radio and television personalities—share their testimonies. A card is placed discreetly on the table asking if the lunch guests would like to meet personally with someone later to discuss Christianity.

These are just a few of the countless ways we can reach out in the marketplace with the Gospel. I believe that if we will take the principles found in this book and apply them in the workplace, we can truly see a Jesus revolution and a massive harvest. Remember, however, that evangelism is just the beginning. God wants us to transform every area of society—family, business, education, government, the arts, media and the various religions. "The earth is the LORD's, and all its fullness" (Psalm 24:1, NKJV). It is for His glory that we "re-present" Christ—present Him anew through us—in every arena, and bring all honor to His matchless name.

Throughout this book, I have poured out what God has "poured in" since I was called in 1973 to reach the lost through God's love and power. I am asking God to impart that same desire to you, and I know it would be His delight to grant it. The hour is short, and our Father's heart waits expectantly for His sons and daughters to be revealed. One way His children are revealed is when you and I bring them to salvation through the Holy Spirit. May God breathe on the pages of this book and on the fire in your heart to fulfill the mandate of our awesome Lord: "This gospel of the kingdom will be preached in all the world as a witness to all the nations, and then the end will come" (Matthew 24:14, NKJV). Even so, Lord, come quickly.

HOW TO PLANT
A CHURCH

We live in an era in which God is moving quickly to plant churches to establish His Kingdom throughout the earth. Certainly there are no precise formulas for what God is doing in each region or what He may be speaking to your heart if you are called to plant a church. I believe, however, that when God wants to establish something on earth He always speaks through the Spirit first with confirmations, and then uses wisdom in the natural to make it reality. Make use of the incredible books and resources available today on church planting—especially Dr. C. Peter Wagner's book *Church Planting for a Great Harvest*.

Because I believe and have stated in this book that planting churches is possibly the greatest way to evangelize the world, I thought it would be important to include some guidelines. Here to assist you is a brief overview of principles I have found helpful in my church-planting efforts.

Spiritual Considerations

Seek spiritual confirmation about planting a church. Pray. Fast. Listen to the Holy Spirit. Search the Word. The first church-planting initiative in the early Church began with the prophetic direction and initiative of the Holy Spirit, as told in Acts 13.

Consider if you are called to lead a church plant or to be part of a team with others. The call comes through a burden and strong prophetic sense. Gifts must match the calling, and the gifts of faith and leadership are crucial for a potential senior pastor. Dr. David Yonggi Cho, leader of what was until recently the largest church in the world, does not send out a church planter until the planter has fasted for ten days.

Evaluate your character. Seek counsel as to the status of your character. Are you ready for the undertaking? The best intentions and desire without the foundation of character can destroy the work.

Gather your "planting team." Jesus never sent His disciples out alone to witness. It is dangerous to think of planting a church alone! Teams offer the best support, diversity of input, skills and resources.

Seek confirmation and, preferably, be "sent out" by pastors and leaders of your current church or by those having apostolic oversight. It is an awesome thing to go with the spiritual protection and covering and support offered by those walking with the same vision as you. There is a huge difference between your being "sent" versus you simply "went."

Practical Considerations

The following are best done with members of your leadership team so that everyone can help "own the vision" and be a part of the birthing process. This brings cohesiveness to your team and gives momentum to the new birth.

Establish your target group. Whom are you called to reach? Seek God and discuss whom He has placed on your heart as your church's "target group." Is your church called primarily to reach youths, the family community, the inner city, a multiethnic congregation, a campus ministry, "yuppies," those who need a healing center for body, soul and spirit?

Research the demographics. Gain insight as to the demographics of the area you are considering by using the Internet, library, city hall, chamber of commerce, etc. Look for population change. Search out the new growth areas with developments that most likely have not yet established churches.

Find out where different ethnic groups live. Look for youth "hubs." Locate nearby universities or college campuses. Investigate whether or not these facilities are commuter campuses or have dorms. All of this information is helpful in determining where you can most likely draw the mix of people God has placed on your heart to reach.

Do "spiritual mapping." Spiritual mapping is evaluating the past and present spiritual climate and discovering why evil or hindrances exist in a given area. You then have better insight as to what will be your obstacles, how to pray and gain entrance to the area, and what will be your best ministry strategies.

Things to Look For and Do as You "Map"

What do people say is wrong with this city or nation? What are the prevailing bondages (such as alcoholism, drugs, pornography)? What is the prevailing spiritual opposition (such as witchcraft, voodoo)? What are the idols and allegiances (such as money, power, fame)? Where did the problem come from (such as the Gold Rush, the capital city, the founder of the city)?

Ask God what you can do to change things. Pray and do "identificational repentance" (that is, stand in the gap for those who sinned against God in the past and ask Him to forgive and cleanse). Pray and break any curses over the area. Pray about spirits over the area. Seek to join with other pastors and leaders to rebuke and break the spirits over the area. This should not be done alone or naïvely. Work in unity and conjunction with other faith-filled leaders who have authority in the area, as there are strong powers over cities and especially over nations. There are good books available on this subject as well, such as those by Cindy Jacobs and George Otis Jr.

In addition:

Develop a clear philosophy of ministry. A clear philosophy of ministry will help you stay on track with the purpose and direction of the new church. It will also allow those considering membership to determine if they are of the same spiritual "DNA" and vision. This saves time, frustration and disappointment for all concerned. The Word of God states, "Can two walk together, unless they are agreed?" (Amos 3:3, NKJV). The best way to be agreed is to know what you are agreeing upon!

Develop a mission statement. This is a general statement of the purpose of the new church. It is usually a paragraph that outlines the intent of this church and what you believe God is calling you to accomplish overall.

Develop a vision statement specific to your church. This is usually a short statement that summarizes the specific intent of your church. It helps keep your members focused. It also helps anyone hearing it to know your specific focus or heartbeat as a body of believers. Two examples are "Saving souls, making disciples in the power of the Holy Spirit" or "Healing hearts and reaching the wounded with the love of Jesus Christ."

Create a slogan. A slogan is simply a one-line "catch-phrase" that people can easily remember and that easily distinguishes your church from all others. A helpful phrase will provide motivation and interest to attend for both the lost and the saved. Our slogan at Harvest Rock Church is "Passion for Jesus, compassion for the lost."

Define your church's values and priorities. God is no doubt showing you strong desires and strengths in certain areas that must be clarified and defined as to their place and priority in your church. Examples of these include the importance and position of apostolic and prophetic ministries, evangelism, revival, church planting, prayer, worship, the Kingdom of God, the Bible, family, children's ministry, missions, giving and women in ministry.

Define the type of church government you will use. Clarify and agree on the type of government for the church. Examples include apostolic and prophetic oversight, eldership-ruled versus congregational input, and one senior pastor versus a leadership team.

Define the church "culture" desired. Clarify what environment you desire in the church. Will it be traditional or prophetic, Bible church or renewal church, liturgical or free-flowing (as in most of the new apostolic churches)? The values you have determined as a team should help you in these clarifications.

Establish your top ministries as a church. These could be the Sunday morning service, cell groups, growth and reproduction, new members seminar, training and discipleship, signs and wonders, personal ministry, counseling, intercession, etc.

Further Considerations

I conclude this overview with a few further considerations that are absolutely necessary in establishing a new church plant.

Establish intercessory teams. Prayer is foundational to all you will do to begin your church, build your church and maintain your church. Having intercessors is crucial. Begin with the leadership team. Then form another core team of those who are called to prayer and intercession as soon as you are able.

Have a financial plan. Be wise and establish a realistic financial plan. Many pastors are "bivocational," meaning they have other jobs while they are pastoring. It certainly makes the most sense in the formative stages.

Get out the word about the new church. Develop a godly strategy for advertising—perhaps flyers, local newspapers or word of mouth. Also, make sure you have a good website.

Begin as a cell group. I suggest beginning your church as a cell group until you have 45 to 50 adults in the group. When you have that momentum, then consider starting a weekend service and looking for a building.

When it is time, look for a building. Praise God, you are growing! Research your options for a building. The key is location. You need good parking, a good meeting room and rooms for children's ministry. A great nursery is vital.

Bless you. Go forth and reproduce! May your next church plant and those you send out from among you be even greater as He leads. You are helping to hasten His return.

CREATIVE EVANGELISM IDEAS

Servant Evangelism

- Free neighborhood car washes
- Free window cleaning for local businesses
- Free tire-pressure checks
- Water or refreshments at local parks or sporting events

Along with the above activities, include an invitation to visit your church or pass out your favorite tract. Better yet, engage individuals in one-on-one conversations about Christ as appropriate.

- At holidays, take sacks of groceries—turkey, stuffing mix, etc.—to local areas in need. Find a house with children and give them gifts, engaging family members in conversation about Jesus and blessing them as the Lord leads.

Prayer Evangelism

- Visit local shops. Offer to pray for the needs of employees, being careful not to interrupt customers or sales. Return at a later date to ask about answered prayer. Look then for open doors to share the Gospel.
- Have a neighborhood outreach. Go door-to-door in trailer parks, apartments, homes. Mention that you desire to be a blessing to those in your neighborhood and are simply asking if they would like prayer for any physical or financial needs for themselves or a family member. People almost always say yes. If the Spirit leads, share the Gospel. Otherwise, you may want to return to follow up on answered prayer and share the Gospel then.

Power Evangelism, Prophetic Evangelism, Presence Evangelism

- Ask those in public places who are wearing casts, in obvious physical distress, in a wheelchair, etc., if you may pray for them. Without making a scene, pray for God to touch them and heal them. Believe for God's manifest presence to come upon them. If you can tell the Holy Spirit is strongly upon them or they make a comment to that effect, share about your God of power and ask if they would like to meet this Jesus or come and visit your church and learn more.
- Set up booths at state fairs or on the local university campus and offer to do "spiritual readings"—but be

sure to let them know up front that these are Christian prophetic interpretations. This term is vague enough that most people will be interested to see what this is. Assemble a skilled prophetic team to pray and prophesy over these individuals. You will be surprised how many will ask more about Jesus when given an accurate word of knowledge!

- Set up "dream interpretation" booths. In some cases we have been able to have these in malls, coffeehouses and bookstores as well as the venues listed above. Many nonbelievers have dreams that they do not understand and are quite curious about. Again, assemble a team of prophetic believers that hear God accurately and can assist in listening to these guests in a nonreligious, non-judgmental fashion. The Lord often speaks powerfully through these times of vulnerability and allows you access to speak Jesus into their lives.

- For the especially brave, be like the youths of Pastor Bill Johnson's church and others, and set up "glory zones." This is where youths pray together before they go to a mall or public place and bid the presence of the Lord to come to the area where they will be gathered. They pray that the presence of the Lord will be so strong that anyone entering the space will sense it or come under such conviction they will ask what is going on. In one instance in a mall food court, without the youths saying a word, one man in his early thirties was so convicted as he walked past them that he stopped, emptied his pockets of illegal drugs, turned to them and said, "What is this?" They talked with him and led him to the Lord. The glory of God has power. Let God do the work first and you reap the harvest. You must, however, *carry* His glory in order to *bring* it. Reread chapter 16, "Presence Evangelism," regarding worship, soaking and intimacy with the Lord.

217

APPENDIX 3

BEING PERSONALLY FILLED

You might be saying, "I already have the power of the Holy Spirit. I don't need this." Or you might be saying, "This is an answer to prayer. I'm tired of 'working it.' I want fruit! I want to know why I put all this effort into evangelism and never get great results."

In either case, this material will benefit you. Remember the "button" analogy with which we began the book? The Holy Spirit is the "power button" who gives you the God-intended results in evangelism or anything else in your life. You will not see the demonstrations of signs and wonders or have the ease to speak the words of the gracious King without it. Those of us who already have this marvelous gift often need to be refreshed in remembering how to share it with others.

Over the years, I have had the privilege of praying for hundreds of people to receive the infilling of the Holy Spirit. From this experience, I have learned a number of principles that may help you receive or share the power of His Spirit.

Get to Know the Holy Spirit

One of the most anointed and successful healing evangelists of record was the late Katherine Kuhlman. I used to watch her on television and marvel at the way she talked with the Holy Spirit in such a personal way. I knew one of the keys to her effectiveness was her intimate relationship with the third Person of the Trinity. Healing evangelist Benny Hinn also has this kind of intimacy with the Holy Spirit. (I highly recommend his book *Good Morning, Holy Spirit*. I place it among my top 25 life-changing books.) We sometimes treat the Holy Spirit as some kind of "mystical entity"; we need to remind ourselves that the Holy Spirit *is* God.

Like God and Jesus, the Holy Spirit has a distinct personality and being. He has been left with us in Jesus' absence as God's presence on the earth. The Holy Spirit leads and guides us into all truth and teaches us all things. He glorifies the Father, convicts the world of sin, brings sinners to repentance and carries out God's eternal plan. Like Jesus, He is one with the Father, and does nothing except the Father's will.

Recognize Your Need for the Holy Spirit

Many times we do not receive from God simply because we are unwilling to acknowledge that we have a need or to ask for it to be met. That requires humility and being honest about our own limitations. God resists us when we are proud or think we are sufficient in ourselves. Yet He is always ready to give the Holy Spirit to those who ask Him (see Luke 11:13). He wants us to be filled with the Holy Spirit and to function in power as sons and daughters of God.

Billy Graham, who has traveled the world over and seen the condition of the Church as he has brought the Gospel message to untold millions, stated at his first historic crusade in 1949 in Los Angeles that "the greatest need . . . [of] men and women who profess the name of Jesus Christ is to be filled with the Spirit." He is acutely aware that we cannot "do the work of God without supernatural power" (quoted in *Youth Aflame* by Winkie Pratney, Communication Foundation, 1970).

We live in a society that values doing everything for ourselves and considers it weakness to depend on anyone else. Street surveys show, in fact, that most Americans believe that the phrase "God helps those who help themselves" is actually a verse of Scripture! Nothing could be further from the truth. God's offense against the church at Laodicea was that they claimed they had "need of nothing," but they were, in fact, "wretched, miserable, poor, blind, and naked," so the Lord counseled them to buy eye salve so they could see what they were lacking (Revelation 3:17–18, NKJV). In the same manner, God desires for us to remain desperately dependent upon Him through the Holy Spirit. Only then can we really be sure that any initiative we undertake is coming from Him and will be accomplished by His power rather than our own. "So then, those who are in the flesh cannot please God. But you are not in the flesh but in the Spirit, if indeed the Spirit of God dwells in you. Now if anyone does not have the Spirit of Christ, he is not His" (Romans 8:8–9, NKJV).

Hunger and Thirst for the Holy Spirit

Once you recognize your need for the Holy Spirit, hunger and thirst to be filled with Him.

On the last and greatest day of the Feast, Jesus stood and said in a loud voice, "If anyone is thirsty, let him come to me and drink. Whoever believes in me, as the Scripture has said, streams of living water will flow from within him." By this he meant the Spirit, whom those who believed in him were later to receive. Up to that time the Spirit had not been given, since Jesus had not yet been glorified.

John 7:37–39

The Bible says, "Blessed are those who hunger and thirst for righteousness, for they will be filled" (Matthew 5:6). Jesus is saying that He wants us to have great hunger for the things of God, and intense longing for more of His Spirit. Paul implores us in 1 Corinthians to "eagerly desire the greater gifts" and to "desire spiritual gifts" (12:31; 14:1). He is referring to gifts of the Holy Spirit. In Luke 11:9, we are exhorted to ask and keep on asking . . . seek and keep on seeking . . . knock and keep on knocking. The verb tenses denote obvious and continued persistence. Moreover, the Greek translation of this verse refers specifically to asking the Father for the gift of the Holy Spirit.

God loves for us to desire what He has told us we could have. If you are not hungry for more, ask Him to give you the hunger, too. After all, we love because He first loved us. He always initiates any good thing we do. Why would this be any different? Be honest with God in your heart, and He will give you the right desires if your desire is lacking. God had no problem with Jacob's persistence when he wrestled with the angel of the Lord all night and would not let go until the angel blessed him. How much do you really want the things of God?

Surrender Your Control to the Holy Spirit

What I have noticed about many people, especially in this day and age, is that we strive to manage our own lives and make sure we are never "out of control." Those who find it difficult to surrender to Jesus regarding their salvation, usually do not like His becoming "Lord." That means Jesus has ruling power in their everyday lives. It is

221

safe to make a "mental" decision for Christ. But heaven forbid He should touch our hearts or our habits.

In a similar way, people can be afraid of letting the Holy Spirit guide and direct them. I find most often this is because they do not know the Holy Spirit. (I would not want someone I do not know running my life either.) But God is worthy of our trust. And the Holy Spirit is God—awesome, comforting, truthful, yes, but also edifying, safe and full of great delight and satisfaction. Just as trusting Jesus is a step of faith, so is letting the Holy Spirit have His way in us. We must let go, and let Him overshadow us just as Mary did when He announced to her that she would carry the Savior of the world. Otherwise, we will not be able to carry and "birth" the things God has for us. That is the only way we will walk in the mighty power of the Holy Spirit and see the supernatural in our lives and in the lives of others.

Check Your Motives

When addressing the great crowd at Pentecost, Peter declared this boldly: "Repent and be baptized. . . . And you will receive the gift of the Holy Spirit" (Acts 2:38). Again, in Acts 3:19, Peter exhorted: " Repent, then, and turn to God, so that your sins may be wiped out, that times of refreshing may come from the Lord." It is interesting that Peter added that God gives the Holy Spirit "to those who obey him"(Acts 5:32). It was when I really dedicated myself to the Lord that I experienced the power of His Spirit. Let go of any personal motives that are keeping you from the fullness of God.

> Now when the apostles who were at Jerusalem heard that Samaria had received the word of God, they sent Peter and John to them, who, when they had come down, prayed for them that they might receive the Holy Spirit. For as yet He had fallen upon none of them. They had only been baptized

in the name of the Lord Jesus. Then they laid hands on them, and they received the Holy Spirit. And when Simon [the Sorcerer] saw that through the laying on of the apostles' hands the Holy Spirit was given, he offered them money, saying, "Give me this power also, that anyone on whom I lay hands may receive the Holy Spirit." But Peter said to him, "Your money perish with you, because you thought that the gift of God could be purchased with money! You have neither part nor portion in this matter, for your heart is not right in the sight of God. Repent therefore of this your wickedness, and pray God if perhaps the thought of your heart may be forgiven you. For I see that you are poisoned by bitterness and bound by iniquity." Then Simon answered and said, "Pray to the Lord for me, that none of the things which you have spoken may come upon me."

Acts 8:14–24, NKJV

Simon the Sorcerer had just become a believer and been baptized when he saw something of great value. His unrenewed heart coveted this powerful gift of God. He saw it not as ministry, but as power he wanted for selfish reasons. He offered to buy it.

The Holy Spirit is not for sale. The Holy Spirit is God. He will give you His gift, but He will never sell it. Ask the Lord to help you search your heart and make sure your motives are right.

The Holy Spirit is not given to make us look better or to give us personal power for our own exaltation, but to glorify God. If any wrong motives are revealed, repent and ask God to forgive and restore to you a right heart. He is ready and willing to do so.

Ask in Faith and Receive

Father God longs to give us the Holy Spirit. Jesus said that if we, being evil, know how to give good gifts to our children, how much more will our Father in heaven give the Holy Spirit to those who ask Him (see Luke 11:13). If we get excited when we give our children something we know they will enjoy, imagine the thrill of God's heart when He gives us something wonderful. This is a gift He intended for all His children to have if they will only ask.

There is no doubt that when you ask you will receive, because it is God Himself who made the promise. Much like salvation, if you ask in faith, you will receive. You do not have to beg God—especially when He gave a command for us to "be filled with the Spirit" (Ephesians 5:18). That is proof He will fill you. He would never order you to do something that He would not empower you to do.

Some people find that when they remove their mental obstacles to being filled, they are filled without even asking.

Your Personal Encounter

As you receive the Holy Spirit, it is important (as with anything else God gives) not to compare your experience with anyone else's. God made every individual unique; what happens to one person may not happen the same way to another. When the Holy Spirit came upon Jesus, He settled as a gentle dove. When He came upon the disciples in the Upper Room, He came as a mighty rushing wind. The book of John tells us, "The wind blows where it wishes, and you hear the sound of it, but cannot tell where it comes from and where it goes. So is everyone who is born of the Spirit" (John 3:8, NKJV). Rarely are two experiences with the Holy Spirit exactly alike.

Also, be led by the Lord about how you should receive the gift of the Holy Spirit. God may lead you to receive an impartation of the Holy Spirit through the laying on of hands as did the believers in Samaria in Acts 8:17. One of my good friends grew up in a church that did not believe in the baptism with the Holy Spirit. He was hungry for something more, so he went to a nearby Pentecostal church and asked one of their ministry team members to pray for him. He received the gift and was exuberantly never the same.

At Harvest Rock Church we have a ministry team that prays every Sunday for anyone desiring to be filled with the Holy Spirit. Because the atmosphere of the church is charged with the loving presence of the Spirit, it seems very easy for the people who pray to receive the gift.

Sometimes we need to go to a church or prayer group where the Holy Spirit is welcomed and experienced, and the climate of the spiritual atmosphere is overflowing with the Holy Spirit. That makes it so much easier for Him to fill you than to be in a church or place that is dry or unbelieving in the gifts. Think of it like going to a well to draw water. If the well is dry, it is difficult. If the well is filled to the brim, it is easy. I ask you: How desperate are you for the Holy Spirit? God is ready to fill you if you are ready to ask. You can go to a spirit-filled church and ask for prayer, or you can believe He will fill you right now as you pray this prayer:

> Father, I come to You in Jesus' mighty name. I confess my sins and repent of them. I surrender myself afresh to You. I acknowledge You as the Lord of my life and surrender all control to You. Your Word says that if I ask, I will receive. It says that You, heavenly Father, delight to give the Holy Spirit to those who ask You. I ask You right now to baptize me with Your Holy Spirit. Fill me with Your Spirit. Grant me the power of the Holy Spirit to do Your work in His power and love and to bring You all the glory. Thank You, God. In Jesus' name, I pray. Amen.

Now that you have asked and received the Holy Spirit by faith, or are already walking in His power, you have the foundation for moving in exponentially more powerful evangelism.

APPENDIX 4

THE WITNESS OF ONE
LITTLE MAN

I heard this amazing true story through the ministry of Ray Comfort and Living Waters. (For information about the evangelism resources of his ministry, please check the website: www.LivingWaters.com.) This shows how each one of us can have astonishing evangelistic impact, if that is the desire of our hearts.

A number of years ago in a Baptist church in southern London, the service was coming to an end when a stranger stood up in the back and asked if he could share his testimony. The pastor gave his approval and the man began to share.

"I used to live in Sydney, Australia," he said. "A few months back, I went to visit my relatives there. I was walking down George Street (which is a famous street that goes from the business district of Sydney down to the rocks of the colonial area), when a strange little white-haired man stepped out of a shop doorway, put a pamphlet in my hand, and asked me, 'Excuse me sir, are you saved? If you die tonight are you going to heaven?' I was astounded by what he asked. I thought of his words all the way back to London. I called up a friend who lives in this area and that friend led me to Christ. And I am a Christian. My friend told me about this church and that is how I got here."

The next week, that Baptist pastor flew to Adelaide, Australia. Ten days later, he spoke at a conference. At one point a woman came to him for counseling, and he asked where she stood with Christ. She said, "I used to live in Sydney. A few months ago I was visiting some friends and doing some shopping on George Street. A strange little white-haired man came out of a doorway toward me. He gave me a pamphlet and asked me if I was saved. He said, 'If you die tonight are you going to heaven?' I was disturbed by these words. I came back to Adelaide and I knew this church was on the next block from where I live. I sought out the pastor and he led me to Christ. Yes, sir, I am a Christian."

Now this London pastor was really puzzled. He had heard the same testimony from two people within two weeks. From Adelaide he flew to Perth to speak at another Baptist church. After the teaching series was over the senior elder took this pastor out to a meal. The London pastor asked the elder how he came to know Christ. The man explained that he had grown up in the church and been involved in the Boys Brigade, but he never gave his life to the Lord. "I became a successful businessman," he said. "Three years ago I was on a business trip in Sydney. As I was walking down George Street, an obnoxious little man with white hair accosted me, gave me a religious pamphlet and asked if I was saved. He said, 'If you die tonight are you going to heaven?' I tried to tell him that I was a Baptist elder! He wouldn't listen to me. All the way back to Perth I was seething in anger. I told my pastor what happened thinking that my pastor would sympathize with me, but he agreed with the little man! He told me that he didn't think I was saved and led me to the Lord."

This London pastor then flew back to the United Kingdom where he spoke at the Keswick Convention, and he shared these remarkable testimonies. After the message, four elderly pastors came up to him and said, "We all got saved between twenty-five and thirty-five years ago by the same person who gave us tracts and asked us the same questions."

The following week, the London pastor flew to the Caribbean for a similar Keswick Convention. This time he was speaking to missionaries and told them about these extraordinary testimonies. Afterward three missionaries came to him and said, "We all got saved between fifteen and twenty-five years ago through the same little man's witness."

Coming back from the convention, on his way back to London, the pastor stopped in Atlanta, Georgia, to speak at a Naval chaplains' convention; more than one thousand chaplains were there. The chaplain general took the pastor out to lunch, and the pastor asked the chaplain how he came to know Christ. The chaplain explained that he had been a reprobate sailor. "We were doing exercises in Southeast Asia and we docked in Sydney harbor to re-supply our ship. I went out with my friends, got blind drunk and got on the wrong bus. It dropped me off at George Street. As I got off the bus this elderly white-haired man jumped in front of me. I thought he was a ghost. He gave me a pamphlet and asked if I was saved. Then he asked me, 'If you die tonight, are you going to heaven?' The fear of God hit me. I was shocked sober. I ran back to the battleship and sought out the chaplain who led me to Christ. He started to train me and soon I went into ministry. Now I am the overseer of more than a thousand chaplains, and we are bent on leading souls to Christ."

Six months later, that London preacher flew to a remote corner of northeast India to give a conference for five thousand Indian missionaries. After the meeting, the Indian pastor who was hosting the conference took the pastor to his home for a simple meal. The London pastor asked his host how he had come to Christ. He said, "I was a Hindu, and I had a very privileged position. As a diplomat I traveled the world. One bout of diplomatic service led me to Sydney. I was doing some last minute shopping on George Street when a little man with white hair offered me a pamphlet and said, 'Excuse me sir, are you saved? If you die tonight are you going to heaven?' I thanked him very much, but what he had said disturbed me. I sought out the Hindu priest but he couldn't help me. He recommended that I see a Christian missionary just to satisfy my curiosity. That was 'fatal' advice. The missionary led me to the Lord. I quit Hinduism immediately and began to study for the ministry. I left the diplomatic service. Now I am in charge of these thousands of missionaries and we are winning hundreds of thousands to Christ."

Well, eight months later the London pastor was speaking in Sydney. He asked the host pastor if he knew a little man who passed out tracts on George Street. He said, "I do. His name is Mr. Genor. I don't think he does it any more, though; he is too frail and elderly." The London pastor said that he would like to meet him. Two nights later they went to a small apartment and knocked on the door. A tiny frail little man, Mr. Genor, invited them in and served them tea. As they were drinking their tea, the London pastor began to share with Mr. Genor all the accounts and testimonies that he had heard about his ministry.

The old man sat there listening, his eyes filling with tears. He said, "My story goes like this. I was a sailor on an Australian war ship. I lived a reprobate life. And in a crisis, I really hit the wall. One of my colleagues was there to help me, and he led me to Christ. The change was so dramatic and I was so grateful that I made a promise to God that I would share Jesus with at least ten people a day as God gave me strength. I wasn't perfect, but for the most part for the past forty years I kept the commitment. In my retirement, I started to share on George Street because I thought that was the best street—hundreds of shoppers visited it every day. I have never heard until now of one person who came to Christ."

A quick math count shows that he witnessed to some 146,100 people during those forty years. That faithfulness has to come from the love of God. You cannot make that kind of commitment and keep going without knowing the results without the love of Christ motivating you. And goodness knows how many more came to Jesus through the thousands of people he had witnessed to.

Mr. Genor died two weeks later. Nobody on earth except a little group of Southern Baptists knew about Mr. Genor, but can you imagine the fanfare he went home to when he arrived in glory!

BIBLIOGRAPHY

Abraham, William J. *The Logic of Evangelism*. Grand Rapids: Eerdmans, 1989.

Ahn, Ché. *How to Pray for Healing*. Ventura, Calif.: Regal, 2004.

———. *Into the Fire*. Ventura, Calif.: Regal, 1988.

Aldrich, Joseph C. *Gentle Persuasion*. Portland, Ore.: Multnomah, 1988.

———. *Life-Style Evangelism*. Portland, Ore.: Multnomah, 1981.

Anderson, Leith. *A Church for the 21st Century*. Minneapolis: Bethany, 1992.

Anderson, Ray S. *Ministry on the Fireline*. Downers Grove, Ill.: InterVarsity, 1987.

Baker, Rolland and Heidi. *Always Enough*. Grand Rapids: Chosen, 2003.

Bakke, Ray. *The Urban Christian*. Downers Grove, Ill.: InterVarsity, 1987.

Barna, George. *Absolute Confusion: The Barna Report 1993*. Ventura, Calif.: Regal, 1993.

Callahan, Kennon L. *Effective Church Leadership*. San Francisco: Harper & Row, 1990.

Chantry, Walter J. *Today's Gospel: Authentic or Synthetic?* London: Banner of Truth, 1970.

Clinton, J. Robert. *The Making of a Leader*. Colorado Springs: NavPress, 1988.

Coleman, Robert E. *The Master Plan of Evangelism*. Westwood, N.J.: Revell, 1987.

Colson, Charles. *The Body*. Dallas: Word, 1992.

Cook, Jerry. *Love, Acceptance and Forgiveness*. Ventura, Calif.: Regal, 1979.

Cunningham, Loren. *Daring to Live on the Edge*. Seattle: YWAM, 1991.

Epstein, Daniel Mark. *Sister Aimee*. Orlando: Harcourt Brace Jovanovich, 1993.

Finney, Charles G. *Memoirs of Rev. Charles G. Finney*. New York: Revell, 1876.

———. *Revival Lectures*. New York: Revell, date unknown.

Foster, Richard. *Celebration of Discipline*. New York: Harper & Row, 1978.

George, Carl F. *Prepare Your Church for the Future*. Grand Rapids: Revell, 1991.

Gibbs, Eddie. *Winning Them Back*. Tunbridge Wells, England: Monarch, 1993.

Green, Michael. *Evangelism in the Early Church*. Grand Rapids: Eerdmans, 1970.

———. *Evangelism through the Local Church*. Nashville: Nelson, 1992.

Greenleaf, Robert K. *Servant Leadership*. New York: Paulist Press, 1977.

Hendricks, Howard G. *Say It with Love*. Wheaton, Ill.: Victor, 1972.

Hinn, Benny. *Good Morning, Holy Spirit*. Nashville: Nelson, 2004.

Houston, Sterling W. *Crusade Evangelism and the Local Church*. Minneapolis: World Wide, 1984.

Hull, Bill. *The Disciple-Making Pastor*. Old Tappan, N.J.: Revell, 1988.

Hunter III, George G. *How to Reach Secular People*. Nashville: Abingdon, 1992.

Jacobs, Cindy. *Possessing the Gates of the Enemy*. Tarrytown, N.Y.: Chosen, 1991.

———. *The Supernatural Life*. Ventura, Calif.: Regal, 2005.

Johnson, Bill. *When Heaven Invades Earth*. Shippensburg, Penn.: Destiny Image, 2003.

King, Patricia. *Light Belongs in the Darkness*. Shippensburg, Penn.: Destiny Image, 2005.

Little, Paul E. *How to Give Away Your Faith*. Downers Grove, Ill.: InterVarsity, 1966.

Malphurs, Aubrey. *Planting Growing Churches*. Grand Rapids: Baker, 1992.

Marshall, Catherine. *The Helper*. Lincoln, Va.: Chosen, 1978.

Martin, William. *A Prophet with Honor*. New York: Morrow, 1991.

Maxwell, John. *Developing the Leader Within You*. Nashville: Nelson, 1993.

Miller, Keith. *The Scent of Love*. Waco, Tex.: Word, 1983.

Pawson, David. *The Normal Christian Birth*. London: Hodder & Stoughton, 1989.

Peterson, Jim. *Evangelism as a Lifestyle*. Colorado Springs: NavPress, 1980.

Pippert, Rebecca Manley. *Out of the Salt Shaker*. Downers Grove, Ill.: InterVarsity, 1979.

Pratney, Winkey. *Healing the Land*. Grand Rapids: Chosen, 1993.

———. *Youth Aflame*. Lindale, Tex.: Communication Foundation, 1970.

Ravenhill, Leonard. *Why Revival Tarries*. Minneapolis: Bethany, 1991.

Reinecker, Fritz. *A Linguistic Key to the Greek New Testament*. Grand Rapids: Zondervan, 1976.

Sorge, Bob. *The Fire of God's Love*. Greenwood, Mo.: Oasis House Ministries, 1996.

Strauss, William, and Neil Howe. *Generations*. New York: Morrow, 1991.

Sweeting, George. *Great Quotes and Illustrations*. Waco, Tex.: Word, 1985.

Wagner, C. Peter. *Changing Church*. Ventura, Calif.: Regal, 2004.

———. *Church Planting for a Great Harvest*. Ventura, Calif.: Regal, 1990.

———. *Churches That Pray*. Ventura, Calif.: Regal, 1993.

———. *How to Have a Healing Ministry without Making Your Church Sick*. Ventura, Calif.: Regal, 1988.

———. *Spiritual Power and Church Growth*. Ventura, Calif.: Regal, 1993.

———. *Strategies for Church Growth*. Ventura, Calif.: Regal, 1987.

Willard, Dallas. *The Spirit of the Disciplines*. San Francisco: Harper & Row, 1988.

Wimber, John, with Kevin Springer. *Power Evangelism*. North Pomfret, Vt.: Trafalgar Square, 2000.

INDEX

Ché Ahn and his wife, Sue, are the senior pastors of Harvest Rock Church in Pasadena, California. Ché is also founder and president of Harvest International Ministry, a worldwide apostolic network of more than fifteen hundred churches in more than thirty nations. The ministry's vision is to sweep the globe with the love and power of the Holy Spirit through intimacy with the Father to fulfill the Great Commission and transform lives and nations. Ché and Sue moved from the East Coast in 1984 after Ché received a "Macedonian Call" to Los Angeles in a dream in which God gave him the promise of a great revival outpouring.

Ché received his M.Div. and D.Min. from Fuller Theological Seminary and has played a key role in many strategic local, national and international outreaches to bring unity, diversity and change to the Body of Christ. He served as CEO of The Call, a youth movement that mobilized three generations to massive prayer and fasting for revival in the United States and many other nations. Ché has authored numerous books, and travels extensively throughout the world, bringing apostolic insight with an impartation of renewal, healing, miracles and evangelism.

Ché and Sue have four adult children—Gabriel, Grace, Joy and Mary—who love and serve the Lord.

To find out more about Harvest International Ministry and Harvest Rock Church, please visit www.harvestim.org or www.harvestrockchurch.org.